Contracting on a Capitated Basis

*Managing Risk for
Your Practice*

APA PRACTITIONER'S TOOLBOX SERIES

Contracting on a Capitated Basis

Managing Risk for Your Practice

American Psychological Association Practice Directorate
with
Coopers & Lybrand, LLP

AMERICAN PSYCHOLOGICAL ASSOCIATION
Washington, DC

A Cautionary Note:

This manual was written to serve both as a reference and as a tool to help providers practice more efficiently in a changing, demanding marketplace. The information contained herein is accurate and complete to the best of our knowledge. However, *Contracting on a Capitated Basis: Managing Risk for Your Practice* should be read with the understanding that it is meant as a supplement, not a substitute, for sound legal, accounting, business, or other professional consulting services. When such services are required, the assistance of a competent professional should be sought.

Published by
American Psychological Association
750 First Street, NE
Washington, DC 20002

Copies may be ordered from
APA Order Department
P.O. Box 2710
Hyattsville, MD 20784

Composition and Printing: National Academy Press, Washington, DC
Cover Designer: Leigh Coriale

Library of Congress Cataloging-in-Publication Data
Contracting on a capitated basis : contracting on a capitated basis:
    managing risk for your practice / American Psychological Association
    Practice Directorate with Coopers & Lybrand, L.L.P.
        p.   cm. — (APA Practitioner's toolbox series)
    Includes bibliographical references (p).
    ISBN 1-55798-362-3 (alk. paper)
        1. Psychotherapy—Practice—United States. 2. Insurance, Mental
    health—United States. 3. Managed mental health care—United
    States. 4. Health maintenance organizations—United States.
    I. American Psychological Association. Practice Directorate.
    II. Coopers & Lybrand.   III. Series.
    RC465.6.C657   1996
    362.2'068—dc20   96-23681
                                                            CIP

British Library Cataloguing-In-Publication Data
A CIP record is available from the British Library

Printed in the United States of America
First Edition

Contents

**AMERICAN
PSYCHOLOGICAL
ASSOCIATION**

Dear Colleague:

The American Psychological Association Practice Directorate is pleased to offer <u>Contracting on a Capitated Basis: Managing Risk for Your Practice</u> as one component of the "APA Practitioner's Toolbox Series" written in conjunction with Coopers & Lybrand, L.L.P. This series of books is designed to help the practicing psychologist build a successful practice in an environment which requires attention to an increasingly complex approach to health care, while maintaining the quality of services for which psychology has become known.

New methods for provider reimbursement have accompanied the development of organized systems of care. One of the fastest growing reimbursement methods is capitation, or prepayment to providers for services rendered to a defined population. Implicit in this reimbursement method is the transfer of financial risk to the provider. Under capitation, providers are responsible for the delivery of care and the cost of services regardless of the amount of services utilized.

Capitation theoretically is intended to create incentives for keeping people well by emphasizing prevention and health promotion. This arrangement may also pose an advantage for the provider by increasing the provider's ability to control the provision of care without outside review. For a profession like ours which has for years advocated the ability to provide less costly yet effective alternatives to inpatient care, capitated arrangements provide a chance to demonstrate that ability. Alternatively, however, capitation requires a rigorous and extensive understanding of treatment cost and utilization rates. Should demand for services exceed estimates, the provider nevertheless faces the adverse financial consequences. A significant risk of a capitated arrangement that is inappropriately created or implemented can be financial disincentives to provide necessary care.

It is therefore imperative that psychologists have as much information and data as possible to determine whether a particular capitated arrangement is appropriate and, if so, what provisions can be put in place to minimize both financial and treatment risks. <u>Contracting on a Capitated Basis: Managing Risk for Your Practice</u> is designed to acquaint you with basic concepts of capitation and provide models to help determine whether a particular capitated arrangement is appropriate for you. With this information as a guide, you can decide if capitation is a strategy that will allow successful control over the provision of treatment.

Sincerely,

Russ Newman

Russ Newman, Ph.D., J.D.
Executive Director for Professional Practice

750 First Street, NE
Washington, DC 20002-4242
(202) 336-5913
(202) 336-5797 Fax
(202) 336-6123 TDD

Russ Newman, Ph.D., J.D.
Executive Director
Practice Directorate

Preface

Market forces are changing the way health care is purchased, delivered, and financed in this country. The health care market is undergoing a rapid transformation from a traditional fee-for-service environment to one of managed care. With managed care, health care services are provided by a defined network of providers who are responsible for delivering care. Various forms of new partnerships and organizations have developed to deliver services in this manner. The insurance industry has responded by developing health maintenance organizations, preferred provider organizations, point-of-service plans, and exclusive provider organizations. In the provider community, physicians, hospitals, and other practitioners are forming partnerships to create integrated delivery systems. These organizations are discussed briefly in this text.

The development of the various forms of managed care has been accompanied by changes in how providers are paid for their services. Some reimbursements lead to lower provider income as patient utilization is reduced. New risk-sharing reimbursement approaches give providers greater control of their clinical practices and an opportunity for greater financial gain. Capitation refers to a reimbursement approach that prepays providers for services that might be needed by a defined membership population. Under capitation, providers are responsible for the delivery and management of care within a prepaid budget.

Providers can gain other advantages under capitation. Capitation enables them to take control of and responsibility for delivering services at the most appropriate levels of care. Providers can realize increased revenues under capitation and can better allocate their delivery of services to meet quality needs, balance preventive care services, and help patients benefit from educational services on self-care.

Capitation contracting can occur between a provider and an insurance carrier, health maintenance organization, "carved-out" managed care organization, private managed care network, physician hospital organization, or an integrated delivery system. In the typical approach a provider is offered participation in a managed care organization's network of providers.

Integrated delivery systems allow managed care contracting to take a different turn. Providers join together in an integrated delivery system to offer their services and capabilities to patients. Capitation contracting under these circumstances requires additional knowledge by providers of services, systems, finances, risk bearing, and management requirements. This book addresses issues of integrated managed care contracting on a capitated basis.

Ideally, capitation can free a psychologist from many of the problems of heavy-handed oversight and practice interference common in some managed care systems. In this regard, there are no perfect answers or models of managed care. Financial risk, administrative burdens, and other issues will continue to be a reality of the managed care marketplace. The following pages give the practicing psychologist enough insight and tools to use so that a successful psychological practice can grow and patients can receive the care they need. It also addresses issues that a psychologist might wish to consider when negotiating a contract with a managed care organization.

HOW TO USE THIS GUIDEBOOK

This book is part of the APA Practitioner's Toolbox Series, commissioned by the American Psychological Association's (APA) Practice Directorate to assist its membership in improving their practice dynamics—marketing, financial management, building group practices, selecting information systems, and other pertinent topics. Every effort has been made to focus on practical advice and guidance instead of theory or philosophy. For additional information, a bibliography is included in each book.

The present book provides an overview of capitation and explores its application under managed care for behavioral health care services. The book:

- provides an overview of managed care, describes the organizational structures that might be encountered, and discusses contracting;
- describes the commercial, individual, Medicare, and Medicaid markets;

- assesses provider readiness to accept capitation and explains the process of capitation contracting;
- defines capitation and alternative reimbursement methods;
- provides methodologies for calculating capitation rates; and
- identifies sample capitation rates under typical plan designs.

Also discussed is the impact capitation contracting has had on the health care industry, especially on psychologists. The number of health maintenance organizations, preferred provider organizations, point-of-service plans, and other types of managed care organizations continues to grow as the health care market evolves. Providers are beginning to actively participate in the managed care marketplace by creating integrated delivery systems, which deliver services across all levels of care and in multiple locations. These systems are designed to consume the risks of managing and providing care to patients. New methods of provider reimbursement also have been created to control patient utilization and the cost of services and to share the savings of providing appropriate, cost-sensitive care.

Capitation is one form of provider reimbursement. This book discusses the evolution of managed care and the introduction of capitation as a form of risk sharing. Psychologists will begin to understand the process and financial issues of managed care contracting under a capitated arrangement. Also described are methodologies for calculating capitation rates under typical plan designs. Readers will acquire a better understanding of the current market, a clearer picture of the components and potential of capitation, and suggestions on how psychologists can be successful in this market.

Chapter 1 introduces capitation, managed care, and market reform in behavioral health care. Capitation is the developing method of reimbursement that shifts risk directly to providers. Through the development of integrated delivery systems, psychologists and other practitioners are able to take on risks of capitated payments under managed care contracts. New opportunities are developing for psychologists to take the lead in controlling patient treatment and in improving the quality of care. By understanding the industry and the historical perspectives of change, psychologists will be able to see how they can structure their practices to remain competitive players in the marketplace and under capitation.

Chapter 1 also describes the various types of managed care organizations that psychologists may encounter when negotiating a managed care contract. Health maintenance organizations (HMOs) initiated the managed care evolution. Although HMOs have proven to be effective in controlling costs and patient utilization of services, they limit patients' choice of providers. New managed care organizations have formed to capture market share from HMOs by developing less restrictive programs; these models also are discussed in this chapter.

Finally, Chapter 1 describes the commercial, individual, Medicare, and Medicaid markets. Reform is occurring throughout the public and private sectors. Much of the recent enrollment growth in commercial managed care occurred during the intense national health care reform discussions. Many psychologists decided to begin discussions with managed care systems and participate in new processes to manage the delivery of care. Psychologists have the opportunity to develop programs and approaches that meet the cost concerns of states and, most importantly, the treatment needs of Medicare and Medicaid patients. This chapter discusses the progress that the private and public sectors have made in gaining acceptance as effective managed care programs and the opportunities for psychologists in each of these sectors.

Chapter 2 discusses issues that practitioners need to consider before and during contract negotiations. Signing a capitation contract locks a psychologist into a relationship for a defined period of time. It is important to conduct an initial self-assessment to determine the ability of a solo practitioner or group practice to accept capitation. The Provider Capitation Readiness Assessment given in this chapter can be used to structure the issues and questions that need to be resolved before considering a capitation contract. Once the self-assessment is complete and the decision is made to consider a capitation contract, a structured process of analysis will allow the psychologist to make informed decisions about who to contract with and what to contract for. The four-step process for evaluating managed care contracts involves evaluating the payer, understanding a contract's language, negotiating a contract, and scoring the contract.

Chapter 3 describes the alternative methods of provider reimbursement. With greater provider participation in managed care, capitation and other forms of reimbursement are developing. The transition from a traditional fee-for-service system to capitation is not simple. With capitation, psychologists have a greater potential to restructure delivery systems for all behavioral health care services. How a psychologist is reimbursed clearly affects the practice's revenues and the practitioner's income. A knowledge of reimbursement methods will assist psychologists in contract negotiations.

Chapter 4 describes three primary approaches for psychologists to use when evaluating the economics of their practices and establishing the financial criteria under which a capitation contract is to be signed. Illustrating and understanding how capitation rates are determined will help psychologists apply the same methods to their own practices. They can determine, on their own or with professional legal, tax, accounting, or actuarial assistance, a capitation rate that reflects the current utilization experiences of their practices.

Chapter 5 presents sample capitation rates found under typical plan designs. Although each psychologist will negotiate specific issues during contract negotiations, these sample rates will give psychologists an idea of what to expect. Various factors included in the capitation rate—such as deductibles, copayments, and coinsurance—will affect the final rate. The sample rates given in this chapter are based on typical plan designs.

This guidebook does not advocate a provider reimbursement system, nor does it encourage psychologists toward capitation. It should not be used as the basis for deciding whether or not to enter into a capitation agreement. Instead, it offers useful information on today's health care market and on how providers can adjust their practices to remain competitive. The final decision is up to the individual psychologist, with assistance from competent legal, tax, accounting, and actuarial professionals. This book is designed to provide a market-based context for the development of capitated contracts and to assist psychologists in assessing their readiness for capitation. The objective is twofold: to help practitioners understand how this new method of reimbursement will affect them and to increase both their clinical and financial satisfaction.

Acknowledgments

This book was written by Ronald E. Bachman, FSA, MAAA, Alfred E. Schellhorn, MBA, and Ryowon Kim of Coopers & Lybrand, LLP. Mr. Bachman is the Principal-in-Charge and Mr. Schellhorn and Ms. Kim are Consultants in Coopers & Lybrand's Health and Welfare practice in Atlanta.

The following individuals from both the American Psychological Association and Coopers & Lybrand were instrumental in providing editorial assistance toward the successful completion of this work:

American Psychological Association
Russ Newman, PhD, JD
C. Henry Engleka
Chris Vein
Craig Olswang
Garth Huston

Coopers & Lybrand, LLP
Ronald A. Finch, EdD
Wanda Bishop
Richard J. Irwin. ASA, MAAA

1

Overview of Market Reform, Capitation, and Managed Care

Psychologists HAVE *contracted with managed care organizations for several years. Most of the difficulties encountered have been related to lower fees and restrictive guidelines on the services allowed. With oversight by managed care companies, standards of care have changed and provider autonomy has diminished substantially. Today, market forces continue to impact psychology and the treatment of patients. Membership in managed care organizations continues to grow. This chapter reviews the growth and concepts of managed care and provides a backdrop for market transitions to capitation. Fundamental to understanding capitation is an understanding of risk, which is woven into the chapter.*

This chapter has a threefold purpose: (1) to introduce the concept of capitation, (2) to show the evolution of managed care as a response to market demands, and (3) to give a market-based perspective for the growth of capitation as the increasingly preferred payment mechanism of managed care organizations. Generally, providers who are able to deliver appropriate services and who understand the financial risks associated with delivering care on a capitated basis are well poised to control the delivery of services throughout the continuum of care. Psychologists may be able to use a new approach to managed care by developing integrated delivery systems that accept capitated risk payments. Such systems are provider controlled and permit providers to determine quality standards and practice guidelines and to address cost concerns. Understanding the industry and the historical perspective of the changes that are occurring will allow psychologists to move to the center of control.

MARKET FORCES

To understand the move toward contracting on a capitated basis, providers should understand the influence of economics on health care reform and managed care. Clearly, economics is driving many of the changes.

Market forces are invisible, pernicious, and demanding. At its core, our free market system provides for the allocation of assets. Government regulation, congressional legislation, and judicial decisions can alter the system or at least prevent marketplace excesses. At this time, excesses clearly exist in limited patient access to psychological care, restrictive treatment plans, and reimbursement structures that can discourage quality care. The reality is that the market is changing faster than regulations, legislation, or judicial actions can keep up with.

Intervention by the federal government on a massive scale does not seem likely, although legislative reforms regarding Medicare and Medicaid are. With market-based health care reform moving rapidly, a provider waiting for government solutions may miss the opportunities presented by the changing market. At best, federal government intervention would address market excesses and establish consumer protection legislation. Areas of potential federal involvement include insurance reform, guaranteed issuance of insurance, guaranteed renewal, limitations on preexisting conditions, tort reform, and new programs such as medical savings accounts and premium vouchers. In addition, changes to Medicare, Medicaid, and workers' compensation insurance are developing.

Certain provider-oriented reforms also are possible. For example, quality standards might be set by a national quality board and continuation of treatment may become part of new regulations regarding insurance "portability", requiring insurers to guarantee continued coverage when a person changes employment or location. Patients should have direct access to designated psychologists. It does not seem appropriate or cost conscious for those in need of psychological services to have to go to a primary care physician before accessing behavioral healthcare services. Legislation to address specific open-access and quality concerns is more likely at the state level than the federal level at this time.

Managed care is not being imposed on the country by a select few. No government entity or oligopoly of companies is forcing an unwanted concept. Consumers and payers of health care services are demanding change, and the marketplace is both demanding and responsive. In many cases the market's competitive environment is achieving negotiated rates that no regulatory agency would ever impose on psychologists. An individual psychologist can choose to accept or reject managed care but must realize that consumers are selecting managed care plans and will patronize psychologists who accept such contracts. As significant numbers of potential patients are channeled to psychologists who participate in managed care, the number of remaining potential patients will decrease.

INTRODUCTION TO MANAGED CARE

There is fierce competition among providers for patients and participation in managed care networks. While estimates indicate that 35 million to 40 million people in the United States are uninsured, the remaining 220 million have some form of insurance coverage in a private group or government plan. With health care costs continuing to increase more rapidly than the costs of other goods and services, there is significant pressure to reform the delivery of health care to control costs. These cost control approaches are generically referred to as managed care programs.

For decades health care costs under traditional fee-for-service programs have increased at annual rates that are several times the overall economic growth rate for the country. As a result, most health care payers such as employers and insurers now enlist managed care organizations to provide a better vehicle for quality health care at an affordable cost.

Enrollment in managed care programs— including health maintenance organizations (HMOs), preferred provider organizations (PPOs), point-of-service plans (POSs), and exclusive provider organization plans (EPOs)—has reached unprecedented levels (see Figure 1). (These organizational structures are defined in depth later in this chapter.)

Much of the recent enrollment growth in employer managed care occurred during the intense national health care reform discussions. Even without passage of national health care reform legislation, rapid expansion of managed care beyond the private employers is occurring, with new initiatives under public sector programs, such as Medicare and Medicaid risk contracts and CHAMPUS.

Along with the new managed care arrangements have come new forms

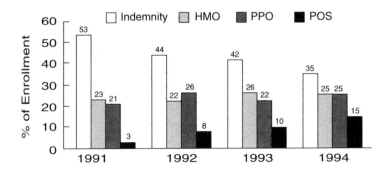

FIGURE 1   Health plan enrollments.

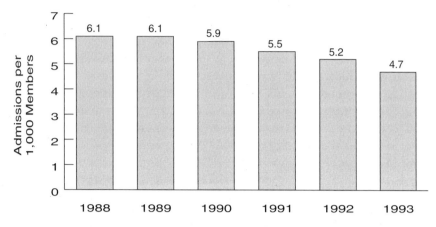

FIGURE 2   Mental health and alcohol and drug abuse admissions per 1,000 members, 1995. Note: Diagram represents national data with a mix of managed care and fee-for-service organizations. Sources: Coopers & Lybrand, LLP; Mutual of Omaha.

of provider reimbursements, including discounted fee-for-service charges, per diems, case rates, and capitation.

Provider participation in the development and management of managed care programs has increased significantly in recent years. Providers are taking control and are now much more aggressive in establishing managed care alternatives that effectively integrate essential resources and control costs. Provider-controlled managed care programs are sometimes called integrated delivery systems. These new initiatives often involve the use of capitation.

LOWERING COSTS

Behavioral healthcare costs and patient utilization rates have been dramatically reduced in recent years. For example, the experience of one large national carrier shows that from 1988 to 1993 inpatient admissions for mental health and substance abuse declined from 6.1 to 4.7 admissions per 1,000 members (see Figure 2). The average length of stay for inpatient care declined from 21.5 days to 13.2 days (see Figure 3). The total number of inpatient days per 1,000 members declined from 131 in 1988 to 62 in 1993 (see Figure 4).

Typical mental health and substance abuse claims costs per member per month in an indemnity plan and fee-for-service delivery system range from $8 to $12. Under a managed behavioral health care program, the

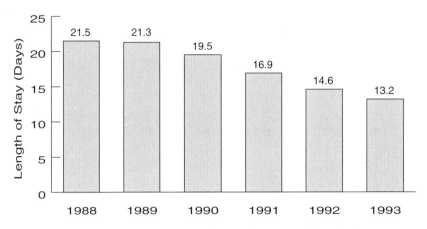

FIGURE 3 Mental health and alcohol and drug abuse average length of stay; inpatient, 1995. Note: Diagram represents national data with a mix of managed care and fee-for-service organizations. Sources: Coopers & Lybrand, LLP; Mutual of Omaha.

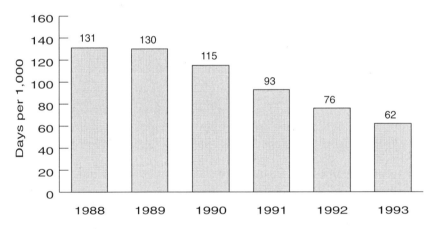

FIGURE 4 Mental health and alcohol and drug abuse inpatient days per 1,000 members, 1995. Note: Diagram represents national data with a mix of managed care and fee-for-service organizations. Sources: Coopers & Lybrand, LLP; Mutual of Omaha.

cost may be reduced to $3 to $5. It is not unusual to see a negotiated rate of less than $3. Clearly, mental health and substance abuse benefits and services have experienced fee and utilization reductions that are greater than those of most any other insured benefit. Nevertheless, psychologists must consider the realities of their business and decide if they can compete, survive, and even thrive in an era of continued changes.

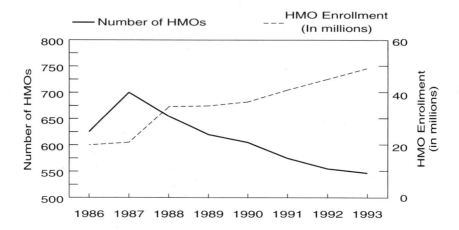

FIGURE 5   HMOs and HMO enrollment. Source: Marion Merrell Dow Inc., *Managed Care Digest, HMO Edition 1994*, p.7.

EXPANDING ENROLLMENTS

Health care purchasers, payers, and providers are aggressively pursuing managed care alternatives that efficiently integrate essential services and control costs. Enrollment in managed care plans continues to reach new heights. Many managed care organizations are creating new systems and structuring smaller networks under alternative arrangements by "right-sizing" or downsizing their existing provider networks.

Nationally, market forces are encouraging the health care industry to quickly address issues of oversupply, particularly the number of hospital beds and certain medical/professional categories. Providers are seeing fewer patients in the traditional fee-for-service system, as managed care program enrollments increase. Providers who do not now participate in managed care may find that the number of opportunities to join managed care networks in their communities is declining as networks gain market share and no longer accept new practitioners.

Consolidated HMOs have led to fewer companies, but HMO enroll-ment continues to grow, with 1994 membership exceeding 55 million (see Figure 5). Despite resistance by some medical/surgical and behavioral healthcare providers alike, managed care continues to enjoy customer sat-isfaction by most payers and patients and is increasing in membership rapidly. Capitation is the developing method of reimbursement to shift risk directly to providers. The key to capitation is to control as much of the payment for the continuum of care as possible.

CAPITATION

Capitation is a method of payment for health care services whereby the provider accepts a fixed amount of payment per subscriber, per period of time, in return for providing specified services. Capitation usually has substantial financial risks for the practitioner. As "gatekeepers" to a system of care, primary care providers (PCPs) may have a financial interest in limiting the use of specialty providers and inpatient services. These risk-sharing approaches include a total or global capitation payment to a controlling PCP group. PCP groups then contract with other providers, including psychologists and other behavioral healthcare providers.

In other cases a hospital system such as a physician-hospital organization (PHO) or a separate managed care company may accept global capitation and hold contractual relationships with other providers. Whoever holds contracts with providers is in the position to assume risk, accept capitation, and ultimately profit from improved cost of care.

In most states an HMO license is required to accept capitation. An HMO license may be owned by the entity taking a global capitation, or the arrangement may be part of a partnership between an unlicensed provider and a licensed HMO.

Individual practices under capitation typically accept risk through the insurance carrier's HMO license. The HMO retains the ultimate risk. That is, if the provider, for whatever reason, is unable to provide care (e.g., death, bankruptcy), the HMO must pay for another provider to care for the member. Insurance laws are set by state insurance commissioners. Providers should seek legal counsel and check with their state department of insurance before finalizing a capitation agreement. In some states, psychologists can directly accept capitation through a single-specialty HMO license. Where an HMO license is required, the contractual relationship with capitating psychologists must include language that ensures that the ultimate risk lies with the HMO regardless of the financial arrangement.

FINANCIAL RISK

In capitation, risk is typically defined by the financial risk a practitioner undertakes with a contract. Capitation is a fixed prepayment for a defined set of services. For that price the practitioner must deliver all appropriate services and is financially responsible for the successful treatment outcome. This means that the cost for any unnecessary services is borne entirely by the practitioner.

Risk management refers to a practitioner's ability to manage and deliver appropriate care within defined financial boundaries. Unfortunately, newcomers to capitation frequently misunderstand its financial incentives by thinking that care must be denied to break even or to profit from a contract. However, capitation financially ensures that a provider consider the overall health of the patient and deliver care in the most appropriate and least restrictive setting. For example, if a patient can be successfully treated in a partial hospitalization and structured living program rather than with inpatient care, the practitioner will save the difference in cost between the two programs. However, if inpatient care is truly required but denied by the practitioner and the patient is admitted under emergency conditions, costs for all professional services are borne by the practitioner. Capitation requires the *practitioner*, not an outside third party, to make all utilization decisions and to be accountable for a successful outcome.

Actuaries assist in developing capitated rates for practices by estimating utilization rates for a given population. The actual utilization rate of a given population may be higher than projected, however, and the practitioner is professionally and ethically responsible for delivering the required services. To manage fluctuations in utilization and the resulting additional costs, the practitioner may elect to keep a reserve fund. Also, a practitioner should keep track of the difference between actual utilization of services versus expected utilization. If actual utilization is higher than anticipated, prices for services were probably set too low. (This is discussed in greater detail throughout this text; the notion of managing fluctuations in utilization is referred to as risk management. See Chapter 4 for a discussion of actuarial and practical considerations of developing capitation rates.)

By contracting on a capitated basis and shifting the risk for behavioral healthcare services directly to providers, a managed care organization is able to establish a fixed budget per member for such services. If service needs are greater than the assumptions of beneficiary utilization underlying the capitation, the provider suffers the loss through providing increased care under a fixed per-member/per-month (PMPM) revenue contract. Under capitation it is important for psychologists to move from practice guidelines to the study and replication of the best practices of care.

If the current health care services in a particular area have not yet been affected by improved efficiencies, a capitated provider may realize a financial windfall if practice improvements can be implemented rapidly.

On the other hand, if managed care has already pushed psychologists into restrictive practice patterns, generated higher-than-average benefit denials, limited access to proper care, or failed to develop appropriate quality standards, a practitioner may be leery of accepting capitation. Such capitation would only lock in a minimum financial remuneration for such services. The ultimate demand of patients, employers, and members for better services would put the financial burden on the provider. In such a case a practitioner may not be able to provide quality medical care let alone operate a viable practice.

Unfortunately, owing to an overabundance of specialty providers in traditional areas of practice, the question today is not whether a practitioner joins a managed care program but rather how much of his or her business will come from managed care contracts and how best to manage the contractual and financial risks. To many practitioners, having some patients at a low reimbursement rate under less than desirable circumstances is better than having no patients at all.

A recent study (see Table 1) demonstrated the potential impact that lower utilization rates have on specialty areas. In areas fully capitated and experiencing aggressive utilization controls, if current capitation trends continue, up to 74% of psychiatrists will be "surplus" or not needed to meet the expected service demands. Table 1 lists other specialties likely to see reduced demand for services if present trends continue. The surplus in psychiatry can be attributed to dramatically lower rates of inpatient care, the substitution of services by psychologists and social workers, and restricted access by managed care. Psychologists have an opportunity under managed care and capitation to position themselves as providers of

TABLE 1 Physician Surpluses, by Specialty

	Percentage of Surplus Under Capitation
Psychiatry	74.0
General surgery	66.6
Neurosurgery	63.2
Cardiology	57.1
Anesthesiology	55.8
Orthopedics	40.3
Urology	32.8
Ob/Gyn	23.4
Emergency medicine	21.0

choice. Clearly, psychiatry will move aggressively into outpatient psycho-therapy as inpatient utilization rates decline and outpatient medication management techniques and treatments expand. Coordination and coop-eration between psychology and psychiatry may be an important link in establishing integrated delivery systems with the capabilities to provide services across the continuum of care.

These systems are provider developed and provider controlled and will allow psychologists to benefit from lower costs and will provide greater freedom in the practice of psychology for the benefit of patients. Whoever holds contracts with practitioners is in the position to assume risk, to profit from improved costs of care, and to accept capitation. If psychologists do not create integrated delivery systems, others will, and psychologists may become vendors providing a price-sensitive commodity (their services). This "commoditization" of care will likely be both professionally unre-warding and highly competitive because practitioners will be subcon-tracted to systems of care that will dictate treatment protocols and will force them to compete on the basis of price.

Managed care is a response to purchasers' concerns about the high cost of services. The traditional third-party fee-for-service reimbursement arrangement created an expensive system of care, with financial incen-tives for providers to overtreat patients. In some sense it may have re-quired outside entities, such as managed care organizations, to impose change on the health care system. In some areas, such as behavioral health care, such outside control has created excesses that concern those inter-ested in patient care, quality of services, and practitioners' decision-mak-ing autonomy.

The next section discusses the most common managed care systems and how each accepts capitation. If your practice involves a significant portion of managed care, an understanding of the economics of the man-aged care organization and its use of capitated contracting may be helpful. In considering the different structures, note the amount of risk typically accepted by providers. Your comfort level with capitation will rest largely with your ability to accept and manage risk.

ADVANTAGES AND DISADVANTAGES OF MANAGED CARE

Managed care can be defined as any form of health plan that contracts selectively, pays for services under negotiated rates, and channels mem-bers to specified cost-sensitive providers. The term *managed care* does not define who is in control of setting the plan design, the cost of services, the standards of practice, or the selection of providers. The main precepts of managed behavioral health care that have achieved market acceptance (where employers and employees are willing to select and enroll in managed care plans) are selective contracting, credentialing of providers, and requiring preapproval for necessary and appropriate care.

Managed care changes, especially in their early stages, are typically driven more by the cost of health care than concern for the quality of care. This means that in the early stages of change providers are pressured to lower their prices for services and to provide fewer services per patient. Thus, without an increase in the number of patients, the revenues, and the provider's income, are likely to be reduced.

In addition, managed care arrangements usually create restrictive guidelines and control patients' access to care. Typically, these changes have been imposed by managed care organizations on the traditional providers of care. As such, managed care has for many providers, especially psychologists, produced negative effects. Providers have been at the receiving end of negative "market forces" that seem to ignore patient needs, trained expertise, the long-range implications of restrictive services, access, and the impact on quality of discounted services. Ultimately, outcome data will help determine critical pathways and the best practices— the next generation of utilization management.

Capitated arrangements are frequently seen in a variety of organizations, including preferred provider organizations, health maintenance organizations, integrated delivery systems, and point-of-service plans.

Preferred Provider Organizations

A preferred provider organization (PPO) consists of providers who have agreed to participate in a managed care network and discount their fees in exchange for increased patient volume. Patients may choose any practitioner, hospital, or alternative care facility, but a higher payment percentage is allowed for services provided by in-network providers. For example, PPO providers might be paid at 90%, whereas out-of-network providers might be paid at 80% . Thus, patients maintain the choice of in-network or out-of network providers with the understanding that they will pay more to use out-of-network practitioners. These financial incentives are designed to encourage patients to use preferred providers without severely restraining their choices. PPOs are similar to the individual practice association (IPA) model HMO, except that providers affiliated with the PPO retain little, if any, risk. Major characteristics of PPOs include the following:

- Discounted health services. Services are generally provided on a discounted basis from fee-for-service charges. Hospital per diems and diagnostic related groups (DRGs) also may be used.
- Utilization review programs include preadmission certification, continued-stay review, discharge planning, and large claims management.
- Claims processing and financial reporting.
- Limited populations and special services. Some PPOs are targeted to specialty areas. Specialty networks exist in some markets for behavioral healthcare providers, chiropractors, cardiologists, orthopedists, podiatrists, and obstetricians/gynecologists.
- Risk-sharing arrangements. Providers may share risk through the use of "withholds," bonus arrangements, or capitation. Separate or integrated risk pools can be established for practitioners, hospitals, and prescription drugs. (Note: A withhold is a percentage of the capitated fund that is withheld, typically on a monthly basis, either to pay for cost overruns or provide a financial incentive and reward for cost management.)

PPOs have been established by various entities and partnerships. The most common owners of PPOs are insurance companies, including investors and physician/hospital joint ventures; they own most of the PPOs in the United States (347 plans; see Table 2).

TABLE 2   PPO Ownership, by Type

	No. of Plans Owned
Insurance company	347
Independent investor	155
Physician/hospital joint venture	45
Hospital alliance	36
Physician/medical group	32
Hospital	29
Multiownership	21
Third-party administrator	21
Other	78

Source: Hoechst Marion Roussel, Inc., *Managed Care Digest, PPO Edition 1994*, Kansas City, MO, p. 7.

The number of PPO plans grew by 12% to 764 in 1993 from 681 in 1992. Membership in PPOs grew by over 45% from 1993 through 1994 (Marion Merrell Dow, Inc., *Managed Care Digest, PPO Edition 1994*, Kansas City, MO, pp. 2–9).

Increasingly, PPOs are assuming shared or full risk. The percentages of PPOs willing to accept risk in contracts with payers increased to 29% in 1993 from 25% in 1992. As managed care grows, PPOs will increasingly share or accept full risks with insurers or employers (see Table 3).

TABLE 3   Percentage of PPOs Having Risk Contracts with Payers

Type of Owner	Shared-Risk Contracts	Full-Risk Contracts	Other No-Risk Contracts
Employer coalition	20	20	80
HMO	50	8	50
Hospital	29	—	75
Hospital alliance	11	—	89
Independent investor	14	9	80
Insurance company	45	19	52
Multiownership	19	—	81
Physician/hospital joint venture	33	—	67
Physician/medical group	40	16	60
Third-party administration	10	5	86
Other	5	11	90
Combined average	29	12	69

Source: Hoechst Marion Roussel, Inc., *Managed Care Digest, PPO Edition 1994*, Kansas City, MO, p. 9.

Health Maintenance Organizations

While organized health care systems have been in existence in this country since the 1930s (with the creation of prepaid health plans such as Kaiser Permanente in California, the Health Insurance Plan in New York, and the Group Health Cooperative of Puget Sound in Washington), the 1973 Health Maintenance Organization Act provided the first official status for managed care organizations.

The cornerstone of the act was the "dual-choice" provision, which effectively allowed employers to offer managed care coverage to employees through the creation and use of health maintenance organizations (HMOs). An HMO is a health care delivery system that accepts responsibility and financial risk for all medical services for a fixed fee per participant, usually on a monthly basis. The dual-choice mandate thus began the evolution toward today's multifaceted managed care industry. From the first HMOs in California, New York, and the state of Washington, HMOs have spread quickly across the country. Historically, HMOs began in the West and moved East (see Table 4).

TABLE 4   HMO Market Penetrations by Region.

	Percentage of HMO Penetration
Pacific (CA, OR, WA)	33
Mountain (NV, MT, CO)	21
West north central (ND, SD, MO)	17
East north central (WI, IL, OH)	18
South central (TX, OK, AL)	9
Mid-Atlantic (NY, PA, NJ)	21
South-Atlantic (VA, SC, FL)	15
New England (ME, VT, CT)	28

Source: Hoechst Marion Roussel, Inc., *Managed Care Digest, HMO Edition 1994*, Kansas City, MO.

The HMO structure is designed to provide services at the least restrictive level of care that is psychologically and medically appropriate. To remain financially competitive, HMOs try to reduce inpatient utilization. HMOs are often based on the gatekeeper model, which uses a PCP to authorize and direct the provision of all health care services, including psychological services, to members. The PCP receives a fixed monthly capitated payment per enrolled member for primary care services. The PCP is at financial risk if the professional services provided exceed the fixed monthly capitation payment. As a result, outpatient services, including psychotherapy, are preferred over hospitalization. Overall costs for behavioral healthcare are reduced, but more of the remaining money is spent on outpatient services.

An HMO participant may only receive reimbursement for services from providers who participate in the HMO network. In most gatekeeper models all specialty care and referrals (including psychology) must be authorized by the PCP. No benefits are available outside the network. In many cases an HMO's focus on preventive health care services entails limited or no cost-sharing requirements for plan participants.

There are four basic types of HMO models:

- *Individual practice association (IPA)*. In an IPA, solo health care providers agree to designate a percentage of their time to HMO participants but continue to serve other networks and fee-for-service patients. These individual health care professionals provide services in their own offices.

- *Group model*. The group model includes primary care physicians, specialists, and other clinical staff of a large multispecialty group. A group model practice has a contractual relationship with an insurance plan to provide primary and specialty care to enrollees. Participants elect to use the group for all care and referrals for services not provided by the group. The HMO reimburses the group on a capitated basis. Similar to the staff model, bonuses are an important component to providers' compensation.

- *Staff model*. In a staff model, providers receive salaries. Another component of providers' compensation may be bonuses based on the financial performance of the plan (profit sharing). A staff model HMO is usually a self-contained, full-service system. Staff providers deliver care in medical clinics that are owned and operated by the HMO. Some staff model plans own their own hospitals. Although the HMO may be predicated on a capitation basis, salaried practitioners are not typically at financial risk for the services they provide.

- *Network model*. With a network model an HMO contracts directly with primary care providers and specialists. Introduced in the early 1980s, this model was established as more and more plans tried to broaden their appeal and organizational structure by expanding access to additional groups or a network of groups in the plan's community.

Although the number of new HMOs is decreasing, overall membership continues to rise. IPA and group model HMOs are experiencing the fastest gains in enrollment, as shown in Figure 6.

As part of the fee arrangement, an HMO may share an efficiency bonus with network providers. Some form of risk sharing allows the HMO, or any other model that measures outcomes, to reward providers for appropriate treatment. Risk sharing is based on the premise that, if actual costs for delivery of care are below the costs budgeted, providers share in the excess profits.

One type of risk-sharing arrangement is a negotiated fee schedule with

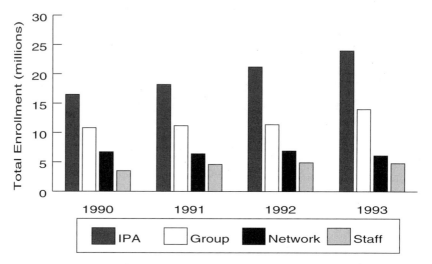

FIGURE 6   HMO enrollment increases by model type, 1990 to 1993. Source: Hoechst Marion Roussel, Inc., *Managed Care Digest, HMO Edition 1994*, Kansas City, MO.

an incentive pool. In such an arrangement, providers are reimbursed on a fee-for-service or scheduled basis, and a portion of the negotiated fee is held back (called a withhold). Typically, a provider is paid a percentage of the fee, such as 80 to 90%, with the remaining portion (the withhold) going into a pool. At the end of the fiscal year, if the plan's experience has been favorable, providers who have met their budget or utilization targets share in the pool.

Risk-sharing arrangements are typically accompanied by quality control and review procedures. Clearly, quality of care is paramount in any system. Provider quality is established through provider profiling based on outcome-driven data. How providers are reimbursed may have an impact on patient's access to care, the availability of services, and the quality of care. Lower costs, better benefits, and an emphasis on preventive care have offset the problems of poor access and restrictive care. However, even with low satisfaction scores for appointment waiting time, office waiting time, and claims processing, managed care plans have a high positive overall consumer satisfaction rating (see Table 5).

Integrated Delivery Systems

New structures and systems of care are being initiated by psychologists to provide not only clinical services but also cost-efficient care with sub-

TABLE 5   Member Satisfaction Survey Results, Percent by Plan Type

	HMO Members	PPO Consumers	Fee-for-service Service Consumers
Overall satisfaction	83	76	77
Access to routine care	80	84	91
Access to urgent care	66	70	79
Appointment waiting time	66	75	76
Office waiting time	60	65	64
Quick claims handling	72	65	67
Courteous claims handling	75	69	73
Range of services	77	73	75
Quick test results	70	73	78
Quality of doctors	81	80	NA
Quality of hospitals	83	84	NA
Location of doctors	82	75	NA
Location of hospitals	75	79	NA

Note: NA means not available
Source: Sachs/Scarborough HealthPlus USA Survey. Reprinted with permission.

stantiated quality outcomes that the public values. These new provider-driven systems that emphasize quality of care can effectively compete with both carrier-driven and existing "carve-out" systems. However, providers must meet the economic challenges and market demands for cost effectiveness. Provider-developed and controlled managed care systems that provide services across the continuum of care are called integrated delivery systems.

Integrated delivery systems can develop and offer any of the carrier-developed products such as HMOs, PPOs, or point-of-service plans. The main difference is that the system originates with the providers, who establish the clinical standards and care needs and bear the financial risks of the system. Integrated delivery systems are often local in nature. Health care continues to be funded with local dollars paid to local providers for local services. As such, direct contracting between employer and provider-established systems of care is growing in popularity and appears to be a natural evolution of managed care. A more detailed discussion of integrated delivery systems can be found in the APA Practitioner's Toolbox Series manual, *Developing an Integrated Delivery System: Organizing a Seamless System of Care.*

Point-of-Service Plans

A POS plan allows its members to choose on an encounter-by-encounter basis, a provider who may or may not be part of an HMO network. Similar to a PPO, additional member cost sharing may be required if an out-of-network provider is chosen. PPOs have a marketing advantage over HMOs for employers who are reluctant to restrict employee choice of providers. To meet the consumer demand for choice, HMOs developed the POS option. To control utilization and costs, a POS plan may require certain benefits (such as preventive care, behavioral health care services, and prescription drugs) to be provided only within the network. Penalties for out-of-network use are designed to offset the loss of network discounts. From 1988 to 1994, POS plans grew from 0% of employee enrollment to 15% nationally (see Figure 7). Most of the growth occurred in 1993 and 1994 as POS plans gained market acceptance.

Many states have regulations against HMOs taking on risks for out-of-network claims except for out-of-area emergencies or when the HMO does not have a specialist in its network. Some states have amended their HMO regulations to allow the broader POS option. These amendments typically require that the HMO:

- maintain higher reserve or surplus funds,
- acquire an insurance company and use it to underwrite the indemnity coverage,

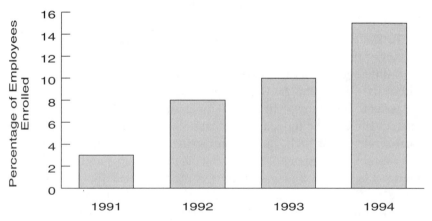

FIGURE 7   Growth in POS plan enrollments.

- enter into a joint venture with an insurance company whereby the insurer would take on the indemnity risk,
- enter into a joint venture with a reinsurer that has a license to write indemnity business, and
- be able to sell to large self-insured employers who take the indemnity risk on a cost-plus basis.

Other Types of Managed Care Organizations

The exclusive provider organization (EPO) is a variation of the PPO in which participants are limited to a closed panel of providers for covered health services. Pure EPOs, with no out-of-network coverage, are allowed in a few states. Some states allow only a maximum differential in plan payments between network and non-network providers. For example, the maximum differential may be a 30% penalty for using a non-network provider. In addition, there may be a minimum plan payment to non-network providers (e.g., 50% coinsurance). The main difference between an HMO and an EPO is that providers are not typically capitated. This type of arrangement is used for large self-insured employers who want to restrict access to a closed panel of providers, who believe their experience will be better than average, who expect continued utilization improvements, and who prefer to retain the insurance risk. (Note: Many large self-insured companies are afforded flexibility in benefit design under the Employee Retirement Income Security Act and therefore are not burdened by state-mandated benefits or state laws and regulations.)

In many communities managed indemnity plans have been the first step toward managed care. Managed indemnity was introduced by traditional group insurance carriers in the early 1980s to control increasing medical costs and growing utilization rates for medical services in fee-for-service arrangements. Managed indemnity is similar to a traditional indemnity or fee-for-service arrangement. The difference is that it involves increased cost control or management of services rendered between the plan and providers.

To oversee the lack of a defined network of providers and the total freedom of choice in a fee-for-service arrangement, employers implement utilization review procedures. Utilization review is a process that manages such areas as inpatient admissions, specialist utilization and referral patterns, precertifications, and second surgical opinions. Patients are not restricted to a network of providers, but they must get preapproval for all

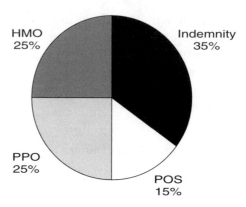

FIGURE 8   Employee enrollment distribution by type of plan, 1994.

inpatient and many outpatient services. Without advance approval, patients may be subject to high deductibles and may risk nonreimbursement. These monitoring and screening mechanisms control the level of care that is approved. For psychologists these controls have created burdensome paperwork and unnecessary administrative work. They also raise serious questions about quality of care and provider autonomy.

Enrollment in managed care programs has reached new heights with the proliferation of new products and organizations. Based on a 1994 survey of employers (see Figure 8), 35% of employees were enrolled in traditional indemnity or fee-for-service plans, 15% were in POS plans, 25% were in PPOs, and 25% were in HMOs.

Managed care systems continue to evolve to meet market demands. Systems built solely on cost reduction and limited access will need to meet patient satisfaction concerns or ultimately risk losing members.

BEHAVIORAL HEALTH "CARVE OUTS"

Most managed behavioral health care companies have been established to contract as separate "carve-out" operations. That is, they bid for employer benefits that are separate and distinct from the managed care networks providing coverage for the employer's medical/surgical benefits. Managed behavioral health care companies either have their own HMO licenses or have established contractual arrangements with HMOs and insurance carriers to carve out behavioral health benefits from employer plans.

In most of these systems psychologists and other behavioral healthcare providers contract with managed care companies. Any profits developed though lower service costs or reduced treatment programs accrue to the managed care company rather than the psychologists. Any equity or ownership interest that exists from the membership base also is an asset of the managed care company.

Psychologists who have established a network of providers may bid directly for employer business, assume carve-out risks from physician/hospital organizations, or accept partnerships with HMOs and insurance carriers. Once the HMO licensing requirements are covered, specialty areas, such as behavioral health, can be carved out and provided by whomever holds the contracts. The most desirable networks include contracts with providers across the continuum of psychological care. Taking total capitation for behavioral health care services, establishing delivery standards, and creating referral patterns together provide a level of control for the delivery of care by psychologists that is not available under current managed care plans. If psychologists do not create such integrated delivery systems, others will, and psychologists may become vendors providing a price-sensitive commodity (his/her clinical services).

ROLE OF PSYCHOLOGISTS

Psychologists have unique strengths to become important players in managed care systems. It is in the area of inpatient behavioral healthcare where the largest utilization and cost reductions have occurred. Fewer services are being provided in inpatient settings. Where possible, alternative outpatient services have become the treatment of choice. As more services are provided in such settings, psychologists can be the providers of choice.

Psychologists are most qualified to provide a broad array of services in an outpatient environment. Services for partial hospitalization and day care programs, for example, may offer new areas for their involvement. According to the Federal government's most recent survey of job prospects for the next 10 years, nearly one-half of the 40 fastest-growing occupations are in the health care field (see Table 6). Psychologists have pay scales that are in the top 25% of the work force. The increased number of jobs predicted parallels the positioning of psychology as the primary behavioral healthcare profession for outpatient and alternate living services.

As individual providers in a broader system of care, psychologists should know and understand the potential impact that accepting a capita-

TABLE 6   "Health Care Reform Won't Shrink the Workforce"

Occupation	% Growth, 1992–2005	No. of Jobs in 2005	Pay Level
Human services worker	136	445,000	High
Physical therapist	88	170,000	Very high
Medical assistant	71	308,000	High
Medical records technologist	62	123,000	High
Occupational therapist	60	64,000	Very high
Respiratory therapist	48	109,000	Very high
Psychologist	48	212,000	Very high
Dental hygienist	43	154,000	High
Registered nurse	42	2,601,000	Very high
Social worker	40	676,000	High
Licensed practical nurse	40	920,000	High

Note: Very high is the top 25% of the work force; High is the second 25%. Pay categories are based on full-time weekly earnings from 1992 payroll figures.

Source: Bureau of Labor Statistics, Washington, DC, 1995.

tion rate may have on the services they provide. Psychologists should consider how capitation rates are calculated and how renewal rates may be negotiated. As providers in a system of care coordinated by a managed care organization, psychologists can provide a wide range of services. Ideally, clear contractual language will specify how they are expected to operate in the system. For example, providers may need to know the following:

- when to expect an incoming referral,
- when to reject/question a referral,
- when to make a referral,
- what services will be provided by the network PCP, and
- when hospital admissions are allowed.

If a psychologist accepts a capitation contract for services that are beyond his or her area of expertise, he or she needs to know how to properly select and contract with other providers to cover the full continuum of care. Providers should understand the services required by each other under any subcapitation arrangement. Finally, a full understanding is needed of what nonbehavioral health care practitioners, such as PCPs, are expected to provide in the way of services to patients needing basic emotional care.

COMMERCIAL, INDIVIDUAL, MEDICARE, AND MEDICAID MARKETS

Patients are typically covered under either a commercial, Medicare, or Medicaid policy. Unless a psychologist builds a practice around self-paying clients, it may be necessary to understand the managed care reforms occurring in all public and private plans. These reforms are affecting the way care is accessed and financed.

Although approximately 35 million to 40 million Americans are uninsured, the remaining 220 million Americans have some form of health care coverage through a private or public plan. Commercial and individual contracts are available from the private sector. Federal and state-run programs such as Medicare and Medicaid are offered to elderly, disabled, and low-income people. Because of costs in the Medicare and Medicaid traditional fee-for-service systems, there is pressure to reform the delivery of care toward that of managed care.

This section reviews commercial, Medicare, and Medicaid contracts as well as efforts to reduce their costs and utilization rates. It also examines the progress of efforts made to establish managed care programs. Finally, it discusses the potential for psychologists to establish integrated delivery systems and opportunities for risk-sharing contracting that exist in each sector.

Commercial Enrollment Contracts

Commercial insurance is a term used for health care coverage that is provided through employer benefit plans. Commercial plans cover the employer's working population and their dependents through insurance companies, HMOs, and Blue Cross/Blue Shield programs. When designing a plan, employers decide if it will be offered to full-time and/or part-time employees, what the benefits will be, the level of employee contributions, and any managed care organizations that will be used or encouraged. That is, HMOs, PPOs, and the other types of managed care organizations that use selected psychologists are made available to employees at the discretion of the employer.

Commercial experience expressed as hospital days per 1,000 members shows dramatic declines from traditional fee-for-service to managed care arrangements (see Figure 9). This is especially true when viewed geographically and by type of system. West Coast managed care systems, particularly those operated by providers, have demonstrated the lowest utilization rates for hospital stays. Including behavioral health, hospital stays

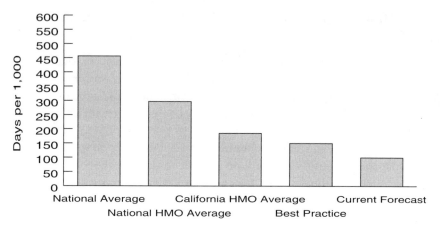

FIGURE 9   Hospital days per 1,000 members for commercial population. Note: "Days" are a combination of behavioral health and medical/surgical hospital days.

per 1,000 members in a fee-for-service plan average 400 to 450 days. In a managed care system the number of hospital days per 1,000 members drops to 250 to 300. And in some West Coast provider-driven systems, the number of hospital days per 1,000 members is below 200. The current industry low or "best practice" is about 150 days.

Provider-driven systems, particularly physician-driven ones, are the most cost efficient. Physician-driven systems allow practitioners to set their own quality and practice guidelines. The need for concurrent utilization management is reduced or eliminated. Freedom of practice is returned to the physician/provider so long as the economic impact is justified, market share can be established, and system assessments through retrospective analysis support the providers' value and compliance with allowed procedures.

The commercial market is an attractive area for psychologists to practice. While managed care has created lower rates, most reimbursements are higher than those for Medicare and Medicaid. In many commercial markets, capitation has become the dominant form of commercial insurance reimbursement.

Individual Insurance Contracts

Individual health insurance policies are typically purchased by people who do not qualify for group, Medicare, or Medicaid coverage. Some states maintain special high-risk insurance pools for individuals who cannot meet the underwriting requirements of some commercial and individual policies.

A declining portion of health care insurance is purchased through individual policies. Most such policies reimburse providers on a fee-for-service basis. Some individual policies are sold on a managed care basis; however, few include capitated arrangements. This is primarily due to the wide geographic dispersion of individuals and the inability to negotiate with providers for lower rates on the basis of volume.

Coverage for behavioral health services in individual policies is usually very low or nonexistent. This is not a market that offers much volume for providers. Many individual contracts are for self-employed people, and most of the services provided are usually self-paid.

Medicare Contracts

Some 35 million Americans are covered by Medicare, which provides insurance to people over age 65 and certain disabled younger individuals. The Medicare program was established in 1965. Despite dramatic changes in reimbursement rates for services provided by both hospitals and providers, the costs of Medicare have continued to rise rapidly.

Capitation programs are expected to be a significant part of Medicare reform under Medicare risk contracts. Medicare risk contracts allow the elderly to choose private insurance plans instead of regular Medicare coverage. These programs provide at least as much coverage as Medicare and typically offer higher benefits at little or no additional cost to members.

As of 1995, less than 10% of the Medicare population was enrolled in Medicare risk contracts or Medicare managed care plans (see Figure 10). The Health Care Financing Administration (HCFA), which oversees Medicare, is reviewing various demonstration projects and studying alternative programs that would encourage Medicare risk contracts. However, efforts to move Medicare recipients into managed care plans have not been successful. Medicare continues to be operated and thought of as a traditional fee-for-service system with the "freedom of choice" as to where and from whom patients receive care.

Growth in Medicare risk contracts is expected to be encouraged by new legislation and regulations providing for more flexible plan options, such as HMOs, PPOs, POS plans, and competitive capitation rates. Today, the Medicare program pays Medicare risk contracts approximately 95% of the local costs of care provided to the elderly population under the

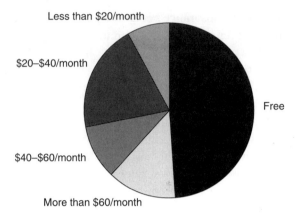

Less than $20/month

$20–$40/month

Free

$40–$60/month

More than $60/month

FIGURE 10   Distribution of Medicare HMO plans that charge additional premiums. Note: Ninety-five percent of HMO plans charge copayments. Information is as of February 1995. Source: 1995 Data Compendium, Health Care Financing Administration, p. 96.

current fee-for-service contracts. These local fees are calculated by the HCFA and are called average area per capita costs (AAPCC).

Managed care organizations can take the capitated rate from HCFA and subcontract with providers, including psychologists. Experience indicates that managed care programs dramatically reduce total hospital days through lower admission rates and shorter lengths of stay. In an unmanaged Medicare population, hospitalization occurs at a rate of about 2,670 days per 1,000 members. In a Medicare risk contract, the experience has been about 1,350 days per 1,000 members. In parts of California some Medicare risk contracts are experiencing utilization rates of about 960 days per 1,000 members. California HMOs exhibit the "best practices" under managed care. Just as managed care organizations have lowered behavioral healthcare costs by driving down utilization, a similar impact is expected for Medicare.

Clearly, a good business opportunity exists for providers while the government continues to pay HMOs and other organizations capitation rates based on fee-for-service costs. Managed care organizations are able to structure systems that require only 1,350 days per 1,000 members. Outside entrepreneurs and other investors unconcerned about provider interests and long-term patient needs have quickly moved to fill the need for managed care. If psychologists are not willing to accept the risks of capitation and the challenge of restructuring the delivery of care, the free market will create other business entities that will.

Some HMOs are able to increase benefits with their managed care savings. The federal government limits the profits allowed under Medicare risk contracts; therefore, many plans add supplemental benefits to the core Medicare coverage (see Table 7). Additional behavioral healthcare benefits have not been common. A window of opportunity exists for psychologists to contract with managed care organizations that have programs that provide additional benefits from Medicare managed care savings.

In 1994 only 3.1 million, or about 9% of Medicare's 35.3 million recipients, were enrolled in some form of managed care plan (see Table 8). With new legislation, a rapid increase is expected.

TABLE 7 HMOs With Added Benefits for Medicare Managed Care Programs

Benefit	% of HMOs with This Benefit
Physical	96
Eye exams	89
Immunizations	86
Ear exams	74
Outpatient prescription drugs	47
Podiatry	35
Dental	34
Health education	25

Source: 1995 Data Compendium, Health Care Financing Administration, p. 96.

TABLE 8 Medicare Managed Care Enrollment, by Year

	No. of Enrollees (millions)	No. Enrolled in Managed Care Plans (millions)	% Enrolled in Managed Care Plans
1992	34.1	2.3	7
1993	34.8	2.7	8
1994	35.3	3.1	9

Source: HCFA, Office of Managed Care.

Medicaid

Medicaid is a major public health care program funded on a combined federal/state basis that provides coverage for the poor. Approximately 34 million Americans are covered by Medicaid. Medicaid eligibility has increased over the years. Traditionally, services have been provided in a fee-for-service market with few restraints on utilization. As a result, total cost increases have strained federal and state budgets (see Figure 11).

Because of Medicaid's impact on most state budgets, states have aggressively sought new ways to control the costs. There are a number of alternative approaches being developed as demonstration projects by the states. As with Medicare, Medicaid changes will include new financing approaches with an emphasis on capitation and risk sharing with providers.

States must get approval from the Federal government before such programs can be implemented. The Federal government has been responsive to requests for demonstration projects and has granted 42 state waivers to normal Medicaid rules and regulations. Waivers granted are usually under Section 1115 or 1915 of the Medicaid Act of 1965. There have been numerous approaches to restructuring Medicaid by the states. Capitation and risk sharing are playing a dominant role as an alternative reimbursement to produce the kind of change that is needed.

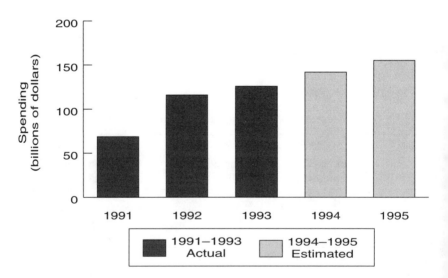

FIGURE 11   Federal and state Medicaid spending growth.

TABLE 9   Hospital Days per 1,000 Members in a Fee-for-Service System Versus a Managed Care Delivery System

	Commercial Insurance Contract	Medicare Contract	Medicaid Contract
Fee-for-service system	456	2,669	924
Managed care system	297	1,352	547
"Best practice"*	133	960	< 400

*West Coast (California) statistics.

Medicaid hospitalization occurs at a rate of 924 days per 1,000 members under a fee-for-service system (see Table 9). Under managed Medicaid programs, the number of hospital days per 1,000 members drops to 549 or less. Medicaid changes offer an opportunity for managed care organizations to lower costs. The economic interests will encourage new business entities to enter the market. Unless psychologists are willing to participate in the creation of these organizations, nonpsychologists will (as occurred to a substantial degree in the commercial market) reap the rewards of lower cost and improved clinical efficiency. Lower Medicaid costs can also mean an expansion of coverage to people currently uninsured.

The core purpose of managed care is to reduce both the unit costs for service and the volume of services provided. Initial demonstration programs have shown that Medicaid managed care is working for purchasers, but change is putting increased stress on the country's health care system. Communication strategies have not produced the comfort level and awareness by participants necessary to use the system wisely, and there have been gaps in access to providers. Also, state-supported hospitals have seen decreases in revenues.

Evidence that Medicaid managed care is working is found in the rise in enrollment in such plans (see Figure 12). Compared to only 9% of Medicare beneficiaries who were enrolled in managed care plans in 1994, 23% of the Medicaid population was enrolled in 1994. And enrollment continues to rise.

Medicaid managed care plans require each participant to select a PCP. Some systems encourage preventive medicine for the eligible population. Despite some skepticism, studies have shown that an increase in PCP access correlates with a reduction in high-cost emergency room treatments for routine care. PCP "gatekeepers" also provide for better care for chronic

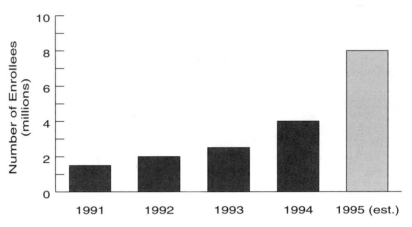

FIGURE 12   Growth in Enrollment in Medicaid managed care plans. Source: Health Care Financing Administration.

diseases such as asthma and diabetes. Additionally, the General Account-ing Office has found that provider access and acceptance of Medicaid pa-tients in managed care programs is slightly better than in traditional Med-icaid fee-for-service arrangements.

While Medicaid managed care enrollment has increased substantially, 93% of expenditures are paid on a fee-for-service basis and are not capitated. First-generation Medicaid managed care programs have tar-geted recipients of Aid to Families with Dependent Children. As the net-works mature, an increased focus on programs that target disabled people, the elderly in nursing homes, and others with complex needs may emerge. These individuals make up a small percentage of the Medicaid population but represent about 70% of the financial expenditures.

With changes in the marketplace, the second-generation Medicaid managed care programs can be expected to follow the lead of the private sector in developing new health care delivery systems that meet the unique needs of the population. Plan designs and specialty "carve-out" programs that target cardiology, prescription drugs, and mental health and substance abuse care may evolve. Psychologists have an opportunity to establish integrated delivery systems for this market. HMOs, managed care organi-zations, and behavioral health care carve-out companies are well posi-tioned to extend their control from the commercial market to the devel-oping managed care Medicaid market (see Figure 13).

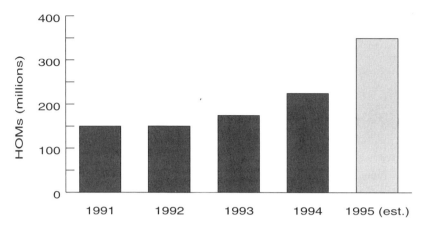

FIGURE 13   Number of HMO plans serving the Medicaid population. Source: Health Care Financing Administration as of June 30, 1995.

SUMMARY

This chapter provides a solid foundation for understanding the unique clinical and financial intricacies of capitation in a managed care environment. An understanding of capitation is incomplete without knowledge of the market-based reforms occurring in all markets. Capitation has become the preferred method of provider reimbursement among payers in both the commercial and the public sectors. A practice's ability to control access to delivery systems and manage the complete care of patients across the behavioral health continuum of care may depend on its ability to contract on a capitated basis.

Reform is occurring throughout the public and private systems of health care coverage. Managed care techniques are a core element of these reforms. Commercial or employer-based enrollment continues to lead the evolution of change. This market-based change has shown dramatically lower costs through reductions in the number of hospital inpatient days.

Hospital utilization rates are lowest in the West Coast provider-driven systems of managed care. Medical practices that support such change are rapidly impacting other parts of the country as "best practices" are incorporated into new areas. The commercial market is a financially attractive area for psychologists to practice. While reimbursements have been reduced from historical levels, commercial payments for services rendered are typically higher than those for Medicare and Medicaid patients.

Individual policies represent a declining portion of the market. Many individual policies are purchased by self-employed people. While managed care contracts are not as prevalent, many individual policies provide very limited behavioral health care benefits.

Government programs are establishing and encouraging new managed care programs that include capitated arrangements for providers. Although Medicare covers 35 million elderly and disabled people, Medicare risk contracts represent less than 10% of this population. A strong push by Congress may increase that market share significantly over the next 5 to 7 years. New flexibilities in coverage and reimbursement arrangements are under review. These changes are designed to bring to the Medicare program the efficiencies developed in the commercial managed care market. Psychologists have an opportunity to capture the lead in offering integrated delivery systems to the elderly. Commercial managed care organizations are well positioned to extend their programs to Medicare.

Medicaid covers 34 million poor Americans under a combined state/federal-financed program. State actions have led to waivers of federal requirements that allow new managed care programs for the Medicaid population. These early demonstration programs show signs of the cost improvements needed. However, the unique needs of this market have not yet been fully understood and served. Each state program experiment is different, but all include some dimension of managed care.

There are large expenditures in the current Medicaid program for behavioral healthcare services. Severely mentally ill people have unique needs. Many people covered under Medicaid previously exhausted their benefits under inadequate commercial plans. Psychologists have an opportunity to develop programs and approaches to meet the cost concerns of states as well as patients' needs. Again, provider-driven integrated care systems can address this opportunity. Existing commercially based managed care organizations are positioned for the Medicaid market.

2

Provider Capitation Readiness and the Process of Contracting with Managed Care Organizations

ONTRACTING, IN ITS BASIC FORM, *is the creation of a partnership. The initial step may include a self-analysis of the readiness of a practice to accept capitation and to function under its rules, requirements, and incentives. Whether providing care in a solo or a group practice, psychologists will want to address fundamental issues of practice organization, finance, treatment process, and information system requirements.*

The process of contracting described here may expose problems or issues that need to be addressed in advance to allow more successful capitation affiliations. The contract relationship defines how a psychologist practices. Patient access—referrals into and out of the psychologist's office—control the flow of business. Financial arrangements, capitation, withholds, and bonuses control the revenue and income of the psychologist. Philosophical compatibility or at least an acceptance of the core conditions of a contract will allow for a successful relationship with a managed care organization.

This chapter presents a structured process for deliberations when considering contracting with managed care organizations. The central issue is: Is my practice (group or solo) able to effectively deliver clinical services according to the terms of a prepaid contract? If so, given the realities of a particular market, the negotiating strength of a practice may be greater or lesser depending on options available to both contracting parties. Many practitioners get caught up in a contract-signing frenzy. Decisions not to contract may be more important to the ultimate success of a practice than signing contracts that undermine the beliefs of the psychologist and the core values of the practice.

PROVIDER CAPITATION READINESS ASSESSMENT

Not all providers are interested in capitation contracts. Many are not prepared to accept capitation reimbursement and assume the additional related responsibilities. This may be especially true for a psychologist working in a group practice with other psychologists, other specialists, or as part of a multispecialty group practice. It may be important for the practice to perform a self-assessment to see how ready it is for capitation, especially before responding to an offer to provide services on a capitated basis or soliciting capitation contracts. To assist in this analysis, a Provider Capitation Readiness Assessment has been developed (see Exhibit 1). While many of the questions presume that the assessment is for a group practice, the issues raised are also important to individual practitioners.

Once a practice has decided to move toward capitation contracting, a review process is important. A detailed review process is fully documented in the APA Practitioner's Toolbox Series manual monograph *Contracting With Organized Delivery Systems: Selecting, Evaluating, and Negotiating Contracts.* This chapter presents a more simplified four-step overview for contract consideration.

If a practice scores high in this assessment, prepaid contracting might be risky at this time. Providers should concentrate on the items with the highest scores because they offer the most significant areas for improvement and preparation for capitated contracting. If the scores indicate that capitation is a favorable option, the practice leader(s) should consider the following process as a strategy for effective contracting.

THE PROCESS OF CONTRACTING

The overall process of evaluating a managed care contract includes the following general steps:

- evaluating the payer,
- understanding the language of the contract,
- negotiating a contract with a managed care organization, and
- "scoring" the contract and signing or rejecting it.

This section reviews each step in a general way, with the exception of the second step. Detailed descriptions of contracting are presented in The APA Practitioner's Toolbox Series manual *Contracting With Organized Delivery Systems: Selecting, Evaluating, and Negotiating Contracts.* Contract language includes descriptions of process, financing, the obligations of each contracting entity and legal responsibilities. The parameters of capitation, such as PMPM (per-member/per-month) rates, utilization assumptions, and scope of services—are subject to negotiation.

Exhibit 1 Provider Capitation Readiness Assessment

Read each item carefully and gauge your responses based on the following scale: (1) agree strongly; (2) agree somewhat; (3) not sure; (4) disagree somewhat; and (5) disagree strongly. Then total the scores and compare them against the evaluation section.

	Agree Strongly	Agree Somewhat	Not Sure	Disagree Somewhat	Disagree Strongly
Organizational Status The providers agree on the strategic goals for the group practice	1	2	3	4	5
The providers' goals include a vision for managed care.	1	2	3	4	5
The providers agree on how revenues will be distributed/ shared	1	2	3	4	5
The "pay-for-performance" systems of the providers are aligned with a managed care environment (i.e., appropriate utilization of services, treatment at appropriate levels of care).	1	2	3	4	5
The compensation of each provider is linked to the financial performance of the group.	1	2	3	4	5
A common set of financial performance indicators is reviewed by all providers periodically.	1	2	3	4	5
The providers have specific agreements on how they will be related financially and operationally.	1	2	3	4	5
The providers have a portion of their compensation linked to utilization management.	1	2	3	4	5
The provider staffing mix matches that needed for managed care.	1	2	3	4	5

continues

Exhibit 1 Continued

	Agree Strongly	Agree Somewhat	Not Sure	Disagree Somewhat	Disagree Strongly
The group supports ambulatory-based care.	1	2	3	4	5
Financial Status					
The providers have arrangements for stop-loss coverage (i.e., insurance protecting the practice against losses beyond a certain amount).	1	2	3	4	5
The providers have compared their average charges and patients' average lengths of stay to the market for the top 10 conditions expected under managed care.	1	2	3	4	5
The providers have evaluated acuity changes due to managed care and their implications.	1	2	3	4	5
The providers can model the financial impact of other (alternative) reimbursement scenarios such as fee-for-service and case rates.	1	2	3	4	5
The providers already operate under other risk-sharing arrangements and understand their implications.	1	2	3	4	5
The providers have determined the size of the managed care population needed to meet their income expectations.	1	2	3	4	5
The providers can compare actual utilization rates and cost of services against practice revenues.	1	2	3	4	5
Information Management Systems Status					
Our information systems maintain and update informa-					

	Agree Strongly	Agree Somewhat	Not Sure	Disagree Somewhat	Disagree Strongly
tion on employer groups, members, benefits, eligibility referral sources, and fee schedules.	1	2	3	4	5
The practice can track utilization statistics for a covered population.	1	2	3	4	5
Economic profiles of each provider can be produced.	1	2	3	4	5
A contract management system is in place.	1	2	3	4	5
Reimbursement agreements are maintained in the information systems.	1	2	3	4	5
Individual provider performance can be profiled annually based on utilization, cost, quality, and patient satisfaction.	1	2	3	4	5

Total Score

Evaluation of Capitation Readiness

Score	Readiness	Recommended Action
23–42	Excellent	Proceed with capitation contracting.
43–60	Good	Continue to improve readiness in specific areas.
61–78	May not be ready	Evaluate questionable areas and correct before proceeding.
79–96	Not quite ready	Carefully identify specific weaknesses and determine if capabilities are attainable with existing resources.
97–115	Not at all ready	May indicate lack of strategy or consensus. Develop a strategy and gain consensus on direction and resources required.

Source: Modified with permission from Towers Perrin, Hospital Capitation Readiness Assessment, July 1995; copyright © Towers Perrin 1995.

Capitated arrangements are important because providers bear the full financial risk. Contract provisions will affect how providers render health care services and, more importantly, what will affect their level of reimbursement.

Step 1: Evaluating the Payer

Psychologists need to know the financial and organizational strengths of the managed care organization it is considering contracting with so as to minimize their risks. The checklist found in The APA Practitioner's Toolbox Series manual *Contracting With Organized Delivery Systems: Selecting, Evaluating, and Negotiating Contracts* highlights recommended areas that providers may research to gain a better understanding of a payer's experience and history.

Probably the most worthwhile analysis of the payer that providers can conduct is to discuss other practitioners' experiences with the payer. It is also useful to check membership growth, timeliness of payments, marketing materials, formal accreditation, annual/financial reports, business plans, and employee turnover.

Step 2: Understanding the Language of the Contract

Contracts range in length, but usually contain the same general provisions, which fall into one of the following categories:

- definition of terms,
- payer and provider responsibilities,
- terms and termination conditions,
- reimbursement methodologies,
- dispute resolutions, or
- claims and other miscellaneous provisions.

Among the various provider reimbursement methods explored in Chapter 1, capitation is one of the more financially risky. Remember, under a capitation arrangement, providers are reimbursed on a fixed per-member/per-month (PMPM) basis regardless of the services provided to patients. Because they are confined to a set monthly reimbursement, assumptions about demographics, inpatient admission rates, average lengths of stay, and profiles of enrollees by age, sex, and other characteristics should be fully understood by practitioners. If practitioners do not understand how a capitated rate is developed, they assume the fee represents a fair price.

An individual psychologist may not provide all types of psychological services, such as child, adolescent, adult, and family counseling, but may be required to provide certain specific services under a capitation agreement. The psychologist will be given a list of services or service codes that can be charged in addition to the capitation payment. It is critical that the psychologist knows what services are contracted. Also, the managed care organization should provide information that describes the interaction between primary care providers and the psychologist. In addition, clear directions are needed on when and how the psychologist may refer patients for psychiatric or inpatient care. The contract should spell out any financial impact or adjustment to the psychologist's capitation rate when such a referral is made.

The following is a list of provisions that are commonly found in managed care capitation contracts:

- *Accuracy in pricing.* Providers are at an advantage in negotiations when they know their own practice revenues and expenses. Specifically, what does a particular service cost (practitioner time and associated overhead is an easy method)? With this information, an actuary can develop a competitive pricing strategy. Chapter 4 gives examples of how these calculations are developed.
- *Services that the contract will capitate and services that need to be subcontracted.* One of the most important questions a psychologist should ask is: For what services am I capitated? The types of services that providers will be capitated for will affect their level of capitation or reimbursement per member per month. Payments are made at a fixed dollar amount per enrolled beneficiary. For example, if the practice capitates for 50,000 enrollees at $3 PMPM, gross revenue will be $150,000 per month. Since capitation is a fixed amount for all services, providers will bear the cost of referrals or other services if they cannot provide the necessary services themselves.

  The contract should define what services are within the scope of the contract and those that are not. Psychologists should assess the financial impact of services being rendered by someone other than the appointed psychologist and how reimbursements would be handled. In general, psychologists should refer patients only to practitioners who share similar clinical philosophies and standards of quality while providing cost sensitive-treatment.

Also, certain services within the scope and license of the psychologist may not be part of the managed care plan design, or the plan's limitations on certain behavioral healthcare services may preclude reimbursement for certain services. Psychologists should understand what services will be reimbursed by the payer.

Example: Practice X is capitated at a rate of $2 PMPM for the delivery of all required outpatient services. Practice X contracts with Practice Y at $2 PMPM for all outpatient services *and* partial hospitalization/structured living services (for which Practice Y must subcontract). Practice X is possibly at greater financial risk in the second contract because it has little control over the delivery of partial hospitalization program services by Practice Y but is financially responsible for its referrals.

- *Unplanned costs in capitation contracts.* Capitation contracts and their associated management and monitoring may create additional operational costs. Investing in a computerized information system to track costs and utilization rates may be worthwhile. Providers should be aware of the administrative burdens required of managing capitated funds and plan accordingly.

Example: Practice X is capitated at $2 PMPM but is only able to distribute $1.70 to the group's practitioners. The indirect costs of managing the risk pools and, as imposed by the contract, accounts for 15% of the gross capitated premium.

Providers should be aware of all possible costs so that they can be incorporated into the final capitation rate on a PMPM basis. Management of risk pools is a frequent cost of doing capitated business. Often, a practice will accept a capitation and place it into a large "risk pool," where, after review of each provider's utilization and patient management patterns, the risk pool will be distributed by a specific formula. Maintenance of such a risk pool is time consuming and requires that a certain percentage of the gross capitation be retained to pay for such services (usually the direct labor costs of accounting for funds).

Capitation rates are periodically renegotiated (usually on an annual basis). Monitoring all revenues, expenses, and utilization rates will help psychologists determine an appropriate total capitation rate.

- *Understanding the payer's calculations and assumptions.* Since the payer (HMO, employer, or carrier) calculates the capitation rate, psychologists need to know what services they are liable for, who controls access to those services, and the assumed number of people covered and their utilization histories. A payer should share its assumptions with the psychologist. Assumptions include the number of inpatient admissions, length of treatments, assumed cost per treatment, administrative costs, and stop-loss premiums.

  Example: Practice X is reimbursed at a defined PMPM payment. The payer's actuaries, in developing the payment, assumed that a typical inpatient length of stay would be 10 days at a cost of $100 per treatment. In reality, the population's length of stay was 12 days and X's costs were $110 per treatment, for a difference of $220 extra per covered person. Practice X is at significant risk with this contract for failing to check and verify the payer's assumptions.

- *Negotiate for unpredicted volume and price guarantees.* What happens to reimbursements when the number of enrollees exceeds the capitation threshold? It is important for psychologists to create multiple hypothetical scenarios to help understand how their reimbursements will be affected. The population may change during the course of the contracted period. Variations in the population mix can be ameliorated to some degree if the capitation rate is adjusted by age/sex each month based on actual enrollment demographics. Actuarially, populations can be adjusted for risk either individually (by age/sex, location, acuity) or by group. Group adjustment requires a retrospective analysis of utilization rates and development of an appropriate adjustment mechanism. This analysis is typically beyond the expertise of most practices. An actuary can be consulted for assistance.

  Example: Practice X included a clause in its capitation contract stating that, if initial utilization for covered services exceeded the payer's projections by a defined percentage, the capitated premium would be adjusted upward. This protected the practice from unexpected fluctuations in utilization rates.

- *Premium changes.* Premiums are set by the payer or insurer. A premium is the amount that employers or individuals prepay for the cost of health care services over a set period of time. HMOs and insurance carriers renegotiate premium costs annually. Trend increases, actual utilization experience adjustments, and other cost assumption changes will alter premiums. Providers should negotiate increases in their capitation rates when an HMO negotiates higher premiums with the insurance carrier. One method of accomplishing this is to base the capitation rate on a percentage of the total plan premium.

Example: Practice X negotiated a clause in its contract that pegs annual premium adjustments to the HMO's adjustments from the insurance carrier. In 1994, for example, the HMO received a 4% increase in premiums and shared a 4% PMPM increase with Practice X.

Step 3: Negotiating the Contract

When contracting, all issues are negotiable. Charges for individual providers and specific needs can be incorporated into the contract. Pricing, administrative requirements, and termination conditions can be changed throughout the bargaining process.

Capitation rates vary by population, plan design, health status of covered members, age, sex, and other factors. For example, a Medicare recipient would likely have a different utilization history than a healthy teenager enrolled in an HMO. Managed care organizations handle all types of populations. When entering a contractual arrangement on a capitated basis, psychologists need to know who their service population will be. Again, the population's historical utilization rates will affect the psychologists' overall capitation rate.

During contract negotiations, providers should check that the managed care organization has a large enough membership base to ensure a minimum level of business per year. Depending on the breadth of services the psychologist can provide, the capitation rate might be based on a membership base of at least 1,000. A larger volume of members is desirable to moderate the effect of intensive and costly services being needed by only a few people. Some form of protection may be available to the psychologist wanting to avoid the financial risk of costly or long-term treatments. For example, in addition to a capitated payment, the MCO might pay discounted rates for services provided beyond 25 visits for an individual patient. Alternatively, certain diagnoses and preventive treatments or tests could be excluded from the capitation. Stop-loss or catastrophic insurance protection might also be available from the payer for a fee.

Step 4: Scoring the Contract

It can be time consuming to review all of the pertinent issues of a contract. Psychologists may not be familiar with the issues and potential areas of concern. Clearly, any contract should be reviewed by legal counsel. Certain items, such as termination procedures, the arbitration process, and financial liabilities, are of particular importance. The APA Practitioner's Toolbox Series manual *Contracting With Organized Delivery Systems: Selecting, Evaluating, and Negotiating Contracts* includes a spreadsheet diskette that allows psychologists to score the elements of a managed care contract. The scoresheet is intended to serve as a managerial guide to assist in contract negotiation and decision making.

With a full understanding of the managed care organization, the provisions of the contract, and the types of other contracts available, it is now time to decide whether to sign the contract. Decisions not to contract may be more important to the ultimate success of a practice than signing contracts that undermine the psychologist's beliefs and core values. In the end, the marketplace will drive the need to contract with managed care organizations. Psychologists are a part of that marketplace and can create alternatives and make choices that impact the developing local managed care market.

SUMMARY

Signing a capitation contract with a managed care organization locks a psychologist into a relationship for a defined period of time. It is important to conduct an initial self-assessment to determine the ability of the practice to accept capitation. The Provider Capitation Readiness Assessment provided in this chapter can help.

Once a self-assessment is complete and a decision has been made to consider a capitated contract, a structured process of analysis will allow the psychologist to make informed decisions about who to contract with and for what. The four-step process includes (1) evaluating the payer, (2) understanding the contract's language, (3) negotiating the contracts, and (4) scoring the contract.

3

Capitation and Alternative Methods of Reimbursement

W HEN CONTRACTING WITH *a managed care organiza-*
tion, choosing a reimbursement method is another impor-
tant decision that providers must make. When contracting with em-
ployers or insurers, providers may or may not have a choice of reim-
bursement methods. However, awareness of possible alternatives may
improve the negotiation strategy.
This chapter describes alternative reimbursement methods, includ-
ing capitation. How a psychologist is reimbursed clearly affects the
practice's revenue and the practitioner's income.

REIMBURSEMENT METHODS

Many HMOs have become financially successful by taking the early
and easy profits available from lowering health care costs. The early stages
of managed care contracting began with discounted fee-for-service charges.
Once cost and utilization efficiencies are achieved, various risk-sharing
approaches are used to encourage further efficiencies through the sharing
of gains with providers. Ultimately, the providers are capitated with full
risk. This final stage usually occurs after most of the inefficiencies have
been eliminated and the associated profits have been taken. Managed
care organizations typically use one or more of the following methods, depending on local market practices:

- *Discounted fee-for-service charges*—a negotiated percentage discount by providers from their usual fee-for-service charges.
- *Fee schedule*—a listing of accepted fees or predetermined monetary
allowances for specific services and procedures. Reimbursement is
the lesser of providers' normal charges or the fixed-fee schedule.

- *Capitation*—a method of payment for services whereby the provider accepts a fixed amount of payment per subscriber, per period of time, in return for providing specified services.
- *Salaries*—fixed amounts paid to practitioners employed full-time by, for example, an HMO. Salaries are not affected by the number of patients seen. Performance bonuses may be part of the compensation package.

Reimbursements for inpatient facilities also have developed variations. Besides some aspects of the methods mentioned above, which are generally used for practitioners, inpatient providers are commonly paid using the following methods:

- *Per diem*—a negotiated daily rate for the delivery of all inpatient hospital services provided in one day regardless of the actual services rendered. Per diems can also be developed by the type of care provided (e.g., one per-diem rate for adult mental health services, another rate for adolescent substance abuse treatment).
- *Per admission*—a fixed payment per admission regardless of diagnosis or condition. Once claims exceed some maximum level, such as the number of inpatient days or total charges, a percentage discount applies.
- *Diagnostic related group (DRG)*—a reimbursement methodology whereby a hospital receives a fixed fee per patient based on the admitting diagnosis regardless of length of stay or number of services rendered. DRGs were originally developed for Medicare patients and are not commonly used for behavioral health conditions.

Provider reimbursement methodologies can vary significantly based on geographical market pressures and the maturity of the provider network. Typically they include combinations of partial capitation, withholds, bonuses, fee schedules, discounted fee charges, and per-diem hospital charges. For some services, "package pricing" (also known as "bundled pricing") has been effectively used to market practitioner and hospital services to managed care companies and directly to employers as a single total amount. With package pricing, providers establish a single aggregate charge for all professional and facility charges based on a given diagnosis or DRG category.

Product line pricing is common in behavioral health, cardiology, oncology, and ophthalmology. Package pricing is usually a precursor to capitation. Since provider reimbursement is crucial in maintaining a successful managed care organization, these reimbursement strategies or methods seek to perform the following key functions:

- provide a steady flow of patients to contracted providers,
- maintain significant provider market share,
- reduce overall utilization for health care services,
- shift utilization to lower-cost settings,
- achieve efficiencies in unit-cost reimbursements,
- streamline the provision of primary care and preventive services,
- use "gatekeepers" to manage referrals to high-cost settings or specialists such as psychologists,
- effectively use the forces of market competition, and
- ultimately shift financial risk for services to providers.

CAPITATION

Various forms of reimbursement were used by the early developers of managed care organizations. Capitation occurs in more mature managed care markets. Eventually, specialty care providers, such as psychologists, cardiologists, orthopedists, or ophthalmologists, are offered capitations. As Figure 14 illustrates, capitation is no longer limited to primary care providers; it has also gained acceptance in multispecialty practices. Managed

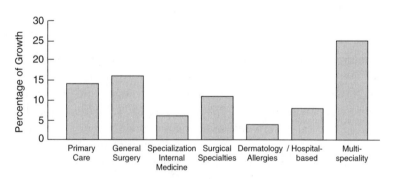

FIGURE 14   Growth in capitated practices by specialty.

TABLE 10   Reimbursement Methods for Specialty Care Providers by Market Size

Market Size	Capitation	Fee for Service	Relative Value Scale	Salary
All	27%	54%	17%	2%
Large (1 milliohn or more	33%	55%	11%	2%
Medium (250,000 to 999,999)	26%	57%	16%	1%
Small (less than 250,000)	26%	51%	21%	3%

Source: *The Interstudy Competitive Edge, Part III: Regional Market Analysis*, Minneapolis, MN, 1995.

care contracting on a capitated basis is growing as an effective way to man-age health care costs and utilization. Reimbursement methods for spe-cialty care providers by market size are listed in Table 10.

One managed care strategy used by employers includes separating or "carving out" certain benefits for special handling and financing. Behav-ioral health care services were among the first to experience the carve-out approach. New managed behavioral health care companies began to promise employers lower costs. Lower costs were easily obtained by reduc-ing the length of inpatient stays and restricting certain outpatient ser-vices. Unfortunately, behavioral health care providers did not establish themselves as lead players in carve-out cost reforms, and new standards and restrictions were imposed on them by outside entities.

Managed care organizations have seen reductions in rates per service and utilization, as well as high profit margins. Managed care organizations in mature markets are attempting to lock in those gains by capitating be-havioral health care providers. In many markets it will be difficult for behavioral health care providers to make additional gains through so-called best practices because services are already at a minimum. However, under global capitation, providers have the responsibility to provide the full continuum of care. With capitation, behavioral health care providers will have greater potential to restructure the delivery of all their services.

There are three general forms of capitation currently in use for se-lected health care services:

- individual provider capitations,
- group practice or subgroup-based capitations, and
- global or networkwide capitations.

Individual Provider Capitations

An individual provider may accept a capitated rate to provide behavioral health care services. This approach is used with providers who are contracting with a managed care organization's delivery system or behavioral health carve-out program. In fragmented markets (ones in which there is little integration of providers in group practices), solo practitioners may be the first to experience capitation contracting as managed care organizations look to them to assume the financial risks of their covered populations. For example, Dr. Jones, a solo practitioner, accepts a capitation contract to provide all eating-disorder services for a given population.

Group Practice-Based Capitations

Many managed care organizations prefer to contract with group practices because they get "one-stop shopping" and a broader range of coverage from groups. Managed care organizations look for horizontal integration of practices; that is, there may be a sufficient number of providers to cover a broad geographical area. In addition, vertical integration is important. Vertical integration means that a group practice includes different specialists (e.g., child, adolescent, and family therapists).

For psychologists building their own integrated delivery system, the one-stop shopping approach provides an attractive package for contracting, receiving better negotiated rates, controlling the quality of services, and keeping referrals within the financial control of the group. For managed care organizations, the ease of single-source contracting and the completeness of a well-structured, quality, multispecialty group practice clearly makes for an attractive partner. Figure 15 shows the percentage of group practices by organizational type.

Global or Networkwide Capitation

Global capitations are generally used by HMOs or other managed care organizations to transfer the entire financial risk of providing care to providers. Employers may also contract directly for specialty services, such as

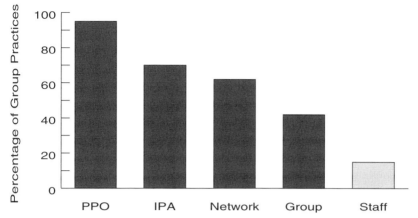

FIGURE 15   Group practices with contracts by type, 1994.

behavioral health care, on a global basis. The legality of a provider group accepting a pure capitation may depend on state law. Some states disallow capitation except through or under an HMO contract. Others require a specialty HMO license (limited capital requirements) before allowing a capitation for selected services. In many states it is illegal for a provider to directly accept a capitation if there is the requirement for substantial financial reserves. State laws and regulatory oversight are lagging market contractual relationships. As such, it is not uncommon for capitation to exist in an area where providers are unaware of, and regulators have not yet discovered, noncomplying contracts. Many providers are simply unaware of the legal restrictions and contract without knowledge of state insurance laws and regulations. Providers should discuss these issues with a knowledgeable attorney.

Psychologists accepting a global capitation do not necessarily have to be of sufficient size or strength to personally deliver all potential services. However, they do need to have established contractual relationships with others in order to provide for a full range of services. Psychologists with contracts for all inpatient and outpatient services are well positioned to bid for global capitations. The larger and more clinically diverse the network of psychologists, the broader the range of services, and the wider the geographical area covered, the more likely a system will be in successfully bidding for global capitations.

With global capitations for behavioral health care, traditional concurrent utilization control measures become unnecessary; outpatient services become very important, and inpatient admissions are minimized. Providers accepting global capitations may be required to supply data on utilization, referrals, inpatient admissions, outcomes, and productivity. In addition, patient satisfaction surveys and other reporting mechanisms may be conducted, with feedback given to individual psychologists. As an incentive to renew the contract, quality standards and outcome guarantees may be conditions of the capitation relationship.

EXPANSION OF CAPITATED APPROACHES

More psychologists are actively seeking ways to deal with managed care organizations. With proper contracting, psychologists are able to maintain greater control of their delivery of care and the financial aspects of their practices. Medicaid managed care programs increasingly involve innovative behavioral health pilot or demonstration programs that are designed to reduce and manage the Medicaid population's escalating health care costs. These program expansions to the uninsured and needy will provide behavioral health care resources to people who previously had no access to health care. Similarly, the number of Medicare risk contracts is growing, and risk-sharing financial arrangements are gaining wider acceptance.

SUMMARY

More managed care systems are moving toward risk-sharing financial arrangements with participating providers. Capitation is a growing method of reimbursement because it mostly shifts financial risk to the providers and thus establishes a provider incentive to eliminate unnecessary care. Full or partial capitation arrangements are likely to expand to more specialty practitioners in the commercial market. These arrangements are considered an important aspect of cost containment in the developing reforms of Medicare and Medicaid.

Many HMOs have become financially successful by taking early and easy profits from lowering health care costs. There are a number of alternative reimbursement methods used by managed care organizations, including discounted fee-for-service arrangements, fee schedules, capitation, and salaries. Hospital payment methods under managed care include per diem, per admission, and diagnostic related groups.

Capitation usually develops as the reimbursement method of choice in the more mature managed care markets. Managed care companies can lock in their profits by transferring risk to providers. However, with capitation, psychologists have a greater potential to restructure the delivery system for all behavioral health care services.

Capitation can be used by individual practices, group practices, or broad-based networks. Psychologists accepting a global capitation do not necessarily have to be of sufficient size or strength to personally deliver all potential services. However, they do need to have established contractual relationships with others to provide a full range of services. Capitation is likely to expand as commercial markets mature and Medicare and Medicaid risk contracts expand into the managed care market.

4

Actuarial Methodologies for Managed Care Capitation Rates

THIS CHAPTER DESCRIBES *three primary approaches for psychologists to evaluate the economics of their practices and to establish the financial criteria under which a capitation contract may be signed. The Aggregate Time Method Analysis, the Buildup by CPT Services Method, and the Market Analysis Method are procedures used to establish the claims cost portion of a capitation rate. Claims costs are the amounts needed to cover the services of psychologists or other behavioral health care providers. Also discussed are other approaches to capitation rate setting and tracking claims experience under a capitation contract. Before turning to these approaches, it is important to understand the components of the basic capitation rate formula. In addition to the capitation for claims costs, total capitation rates should include administrative expenses, stop-loss insurance protection, and a margin for fluctuations in expected experience.*

Capitation Rate =
Claims Cost + Administrative Expenses + Stop-Loss + Margin

CAPITATION CLAIMS COST

Capitation is a method of prepayment to providers for services that may be needed by a defined covered population. Capitation is typically expressed on a PMPM basis, meaning the payer pays a set amount for the covered services per beneficiary (or member). There are a number of ways to develop an acceptable capitation claims cost. The basic concept is simple.

$$\text{Capitation Claims Cost PMPM} = \frac{\text{Annual Frequency} \times \text{Cost}}{12 \times 1,000}$$

Frequency is usually based on historical claims experience that reflects the number of services provided per 1,000 members in a recent year. The cost is the actual price per service provided. Both frequency and costs are changing dramatically in the delivery of behavioral health care services today.

Market competition regarding prices is forcing efficiency changes that in many instances have not yet been implemented by providers or proven in clinical trials. In many markets, capitation may have little to do with the actual costs of providing care and more to do with competitive bidding by providers. Psychologists will need to decide how much they are willing to accept in a capitation agreement, not in terms of historical charges but rather in terms of future expectations. Essentially, how close to your practice's costs are you willing to bid to provide services? The closer your bid, the greater your financial risk.

ACTUARIAL AND PRACTICAL CONSIDERATIONS

Before psychologists can begin to understand actual calculation methods, it is important to review the preliminary actuarial and practical considerations necessary for developing capitation rates. The major areas to consider include the following:

- *Components of capitation.* The five pieces of information used to determine a capitation rate are (1) frequency, (2) cost per encounter/service, (3) administrative expenses, (4) reinsurance or stop-loss costs, and (5) a margin for fluctuations in expected experience. Under a capitated arrangement, psychologists' incomes are affected by the number of and charges per service that they provide to their patients. The number of services provided, referred to as the utilization rate consists of admission rates (number of patients per 1,000 members admitted to treatment programs) and the average length of treatment.

  Capitation calculations are based on data from large groups. Actuaries are able to model the expected utilization of psychological services based on the historical experience of a similar population. It is necessary to use databases with large populations for statistical significance.

Capitation rates should reflect all factors of expected utilization. For example, the rate of beginning services (the admission rate) and the average length of treatment can vary by age, sex, industry, income, and other factors of a group being priced. How a group is selected for coverage based on the above variables is important to the expected utilization. For example, initial screening procedures by managed care underwriters, geographical factors, and marketing factors have an impact on selecting healthy or unhealthy members. Providers should consider hiring an actuary to assist in adjusting the capitated price for individual or group variables as described above. Alternatively, an actuary can assist in evaluating a contract's proposed offering. In negotiating terms, the payer will surely model expected utilization, and the payer's actuary will assign a rate based on the payer's assumptions.

Administrative costs also are incorporated into the capitation rate. These include billing, secretarial services, and marketing. It is desirable to include in the capitation rate a margin for fluctuation. The negotiations between providers and managed care organizations will ultimately determine the inclusion of any margin.

Reinsurance, or stop-loss expenses, may be incorporated into the rate calculation. These terms are sometimes used interchangeably. In reinsurance a third party assumes risk for certain large claims. Stop-loss expenses are used when a managed care organization provides the large claim protection. Arrangements are made to protect the provider from claims risks that the provider cannot easily manage financially. For example, a managed care organization might insure 80 percent of hospital charges that exceed $20,000 for any one patient or total costs exceeding 125% of expected charges.

For a psychologist, stop-loss coverage may provide protection for patients under capitation that need long-term intensive psychotherapy. For example, after 20 to 30 visits in a given year, further payment is permitted based on discounted fees. This would allow for reimbursement in addition to the capitation. This stop-loss or reinsurance protection carries with it a cost that should be figured into the capitation rate.

Exhibit 2 gives a simplified example of the effects of the components mentioned above for outpatient services on a PMPM basis.

EXHIBIT 2   Example Capitation Rate Calculation for Inpatient
Services

No. of admissions for treatment per 1,000 members:	30
Average length of treatment (visits per 1,000 members):	8
Average cost per treatment:	$90
Monthly claim cost: 30 x 8 x 90	
12 x 1,000	$1.80
Administrative costs (5% of claim costs):	$ .09
Profit/margin (2% of claim costs):	$ .04
Reinsurance/stop-loss cost (4% of claim costs):	$ .07
Total PMPM cost: $2.00	

It is assumed that, in a population of 1,000, 30 members will seek outpatient psychotherapy in a year. The average length of treatment is eight visits, and the total cost per visit is $90. Assuming that administrative, margin, and reinsurance/stop-loss costs are 5%, 2%, and 4%, respectively, of the claims cost, the total monthly cost per member for outpatient services is $2.00.

- *Information and data needs.* Gathering as much information as possible about the capitation arrangement is critical for psychologists in determining an accurate capitation rate. Psychologists requesting data and information for calculating capitations should consider the following:

- *Plan design description.* Plan design has a significant impact on calculation of the capitation rate. Providers will receive payment not only from the capitation but also from cost-sharing payments provided by the patients. These cost-sharing payments may include deductibles, copayments, and coinsurance. Deductibles are the sum a patient must pay before an insurer assumes liability for the remaining cost of covered services. Copayments are a type of cost sharing whereby a patient pays a specified amount per unit of service or unit of time (e.g., $10 per visit). Coinsurance is a cost-sharing ratio between the patient (or beneficiary) and the insurer or employer (e.g., the patient pays 20% of covered charges). In general, if a plan's design requires collection of a deductible, copayment, and/or coinsurance by the practitioner, this will probably lower the capitated rate offered. If, for example, a contract specifies a payment of $4 PMPM, the provider should determine whether the plan is actually paying $3 PMPM and expecting the provider to collect the additional $1 through the plan's cost-sharing arrangements. Again, providers should seek professional assistance to model the effect of plan design on their contracts.

Knowing what services are covered under a capitated arrangement is important and has an effect on providers' revenue. Practitioners should fully understand what services they are at financial risk to provide.

- *Interaction between providers.* When financial payments change, as with moving from a fee-for-service arrangement to capitation, who provides what services will also change. Incentives to refer or not to refer also change. For example, in some capitation arrangements, PCPs may be at a financial advantage for referring rapidly to specialists. In other capitation arrangements, referral expenses may reduce the PCP's capitation. In this case, the payer is providing a financial incentive for PCPs to provide as much treatment as is possible and appropriate. As providers, psychologists need to know how utilization will be affected by the financial arrangements of referring providers. In the contract are you considered a specialist or a generalist? What are the financial incentives for referring to another practitioner?

- *Population to be covered.* The makeup of the population that a provider will cover affects the final capitation rate. Commercial, Medicare, and Medicaid populations experience different utilization rates and costs of care. The geographical area in which a covered population resides also affects rates. Since capitation reflects local market costs, it may be higher in urban areas than in rural areas, depending on the costs to perform services and the demand for them. The risk characteristics of the population (e.g., age, sex, retiree status) also affect utilization rates and therefore the capitation rate.

Since the actual experience of a given group of patients is the most credible data, insurers or underwriters will adjust or "experience rate" data according to the population to be covered. If a premium is experience rated, the capitation rate should be tied to the premium adjustments.

- *Utilization data.* As mentioned above, utilization statistics for a provider's practice are an essential component of the capitation rate calculation process. The ideal utilization data reflect that actual experience for a particular provider for a specific population, such as Medicare or Medicaid. To be statistically valid and reflect a practice's utilization experience, the data should usually represent a covered population of at least 1,000. If actual experience data for a provider's practice are not available, other data sources to use include insurance carrier and HMO experience. In many cases a managed care organization will share its historical data. If necessary, the plan manager can provide this information.

Consultants and actuaries also have databases and capitation pricing models that can be used to calculate capitation rates. Federal and state insurance agencies also may have applicable data. Insurance carrier and HMO rate filings with state departments of insurance can include detailed utilization assumptions by procedure. Regardless of the data source used, the key is to use detailed and accurate data that represent characteristics of the desired population and the expected use of services under capitation.

- *Competitive information.* To thrive today, psychologists need to know the economics of their own practices, the strengths and weaknesses of competing practices, the needs of the managed care organization, and the dynamics of the local market. To date, most psychologists have operated as individual practitioners. As integrated delivery systems evolve and exclusive managed care relationships develop, knowledge of the competitive marketplace will provide tactical advantages in contracting for specific capitations and strategic advantages in selecting the right partnerships.

AGGREGATE TIME ANALYSIS

A capitation calculation based on an aggregate time analysis is a starting point for a psychologist to develop a capitation rate. It is based on an internal analysis of the practice and the time required to deliver appropriate services. What determines an acceptable capitation rate for a practitioner are the revenues required by the psychologist to run a successful practice. Modifications to the capitation rate may be required due to market competition, alternative opportunities available to the psychologist, the aggressiveness required to establish market share, the ability of the psychologist to improve existing practice patterns, and the quality of the services delivered. Ultimately, the negotiating strength of the psychologist and the needs of the market will drive the establishment of the capitation.

Exhibit 3 shows a sample analysis of a well-established solo practitioner in a fee-for-service market. With 40 hours of work per week and 52 weeks in a year, the psychologist has 2,080 hours available for professional behavioral health care services for his/her patients, administrative work, marketing, training seminars, and vacations. On average, only 60% of the psychologist's time is actually spent with patients delivering behavioral health services for which a bill is paid. The remaining nonbillable portion (40%) of the psychologist's time includes pro-bono work and uncollectible amounts. Psychologists may want to recognize expected levels of pro-bono work and/or historical levels of uncollected or bad debts separately from other nonbillable hours of vacation, marketing, and training seminars.

Since 60% of the provider's time is actually billable, the psychologist has 1,248 hours of net billable time in a given year (.60 × 2,080). Assuming each visit averages 55 minutes, the psychologist can realistically provide up to 1,361 visits a year.

If the average visit generates $105 (including tests and evaluations), total revenues are estimated by multiplying the revenue per visit by the number of visits, to generate total revenues of $142,905 per year ($105 x 1,361). The $105 per visit includes all payments from insurance carriers and the out-of-pocket costs satisfied by patients. These out-of-pocket costs include copayments, coinsurance, or other forms of cost sharing paid by patients.

Overhead expenses are assumed to be 20% of net revenues and include expenses other than employee benefits, such as secretarial services, utilities, rent, furniture and equipment, administrative costs, postage, and telephone service.

Expenses for benefits are assumed to be 30% of net revenues and include premiums for health insurance, life insurance, disability coverage, workers' compensation, unemployment insurance, and retirement plan funding policies.

Since overhead and benefits expenses are expressed as a percentage of net revenue, the net revenue can be determined by using the following equations:

Total revenue = Net revenue + (.20 x Net revenue) + (.30 x Net revenue)
Total revenue = 1.50 x Net revenue
Net revenue = $\dfrac{\text{Total revenue}}{1.50}$
Net revenue = $\dfrac{\$142{,}905}{1.50}$
Net revenue = $95,270 (annual)

Net revenue is similar to "take-home pay" or a salary. Using the above approach allows a psychologist to determine his/her desired net revenue. Alternative values for net revenue can be calculated by reworking the formula assumptions to reflect actual practice considerations of work hours, overhead, benefits, and average payments for services rendered. Once the analysis is structured to reflect a psychologist's revenue requirements, the process can be extended to a capitation determination.

CAPITATION BY AGGREGATE TIME METHOD

Based on the assumptions made in the example above, which used the aggregate time method, a psychologist can provide 1,361 visits in a 12-month period. For example, from actuarial tables for outpatient psychotherapy visits in many PPO systems, 1,361 visits can be expected from a managed care organization with 5,026 members. This sample covered population typically has a mix of male and female adults and children. In selecting an actuary, a psychologist should ensure that assumptions are specified as to the type of managed care organization and the plan design.

Plan design has a significant impact on the capitation calculation. The psychologist will receive revenue from both the managed care capitation payment and the cost-sharing arrangements required of patients. In this example the plan design for the PPO is as follows:

- Outpatient benefit: 80% coinsurance with an annual maximum of $2,500

EXHIBIT 3 Aggregate Time Analysis

	Basis	Annual Totals
Number of work hours	40 hour per week	2,080 hours
Number of patient hours	60% of weekly work hours	1,248 hours
Number of visits	55 minutes/visit	1,361 visits
Total revenue	$105/visit	$142,905
Overhead (rent, utilities, equipment, etc.)	20% of net revenue	$19,054
Benefits (health, life, disability, etc.)	30% of net revenue	$28,581
Net revenue (after business expenses)		$95,270

EXHIBIT 4   Aggregate Time Method Capitation

	Total Revenues	Copayment Revenues	Capitation Revenues	Capitation PMPM
Psychologist's services	$142,905	$43,886	$99,019	$1.64
All outpatient services	$203,638	$62,517	$141,121	$2.34
All inpatient and outpatient services	$462,311	$99,859	$362,452	$6.01

- Partial hospitalization: $50 daily copayment with an annual maximum of 60 days
- Inpatient hospitalization: $100 daily copayment with an annual maximum of 30 days

Exhibit 4 shows total expected revenues, copayment revenues, capitation revenues, and the subsequent capitation on a PMPM basis for a PPO with 5,026 members, 1,361 visits, and a charge of $105 per visit.

Copayment revenues can be determined from actuarial models provided by the managed care organizations, from data or the historical experience of the practice, or from estimates using similar managed care contracts as a guide. This information should be shared with the provider by the payer since it reflects the provider's total compensation under the capitation contract.

Capitation revenue is total revenue less copayment revenue. That is, the capitation will cover the revenue not otherwise covered by patients. Since all revenues used reflect an annual or 12-month analysis, the capitation revenue can be divided by 12 to determine the monthly capitation amount. Dividing the monthly capitation revenue by the number of members (5,026 in this case) yields the capitation rate on the usual PMPM basis.

Capitation revenue = Total revenue − copayment revenue
Capitation revenue = $142,953 - $43,886
Capitation revenue = $99,067

Monthly capitation revenue = $99,067÷12
Monthly capitation revenue = $8,256
Capitation PMPM =Monthly capitation revenue ÷ number of members
Capitation PMPM = $8,256 ÷ 5,026
Capitation PMPM = $1.64

In this example the practitioner would be paid $1.64 per member per month to provide services for 5,026 beneficiaries, or $8,256 per month.

The capitation rate is typically for all outpatient services within the scope of the psychologist's license (including tests, evaluations, psychotherapy visits). Determining the scope of services to be provided is critical to the success and satisfaction the psychologist will have with the capitation arrangement. The capitation contract should specify which services are expected, under what circumstances, and with what referral authority services will be provided.

The above calculation shows what capitation rate would be necessary for the psychologist to achieve the target annual revenue amount from a single capitation contract. Capitation from any one contract is likely to be only a part of a practice's revenue. A psychologist may have multiple contracts at different capitation rates covering different populations. Based on negotiations, other contract options available, and marketing strategy, a psychologist may agree to contract at lower capitation amounts or bid higher and hope that the managed care company recognizes the quality of the practice's value-added services. A psychologist who bids and receives only low capitation rates may find his or her practice capacity is filled when more desirable contracts are offered by other payers.

Exhibit 4 also shows what the PMPM capitation rates are for all outpatient visits and for all behavioral health care services: $2.34 and $6.01, respectively. In this example the psychologist can contract for his or her services, bid to provide broader services through affiliations or separate contracts with other psychologists, or bid on all outpatient and inpatient services. For example, the psychologist may accept $2.34 PMPM for all outpatient services. To take on that service requirement, the psychologist may contract with other psychologists, psychiatrists, social workers, or other providers to be able to cover all outpatient services.

The controlling psychologist may then "subcapitate" the contracted specialists or pay them on a discounted fee-for-service basis. If the specialists are not subcapitated, the controlling psychologist risks that the capitation rate received ($2.34 PMPM) will not be adequate to cover the costs of all services rendered. In that case the psychologist would suffer the economic loss or realize a reduced payment for his or her own services. The reduction would occur because the psychologist would receive only the remainder of the capitation funds after payment is made to the referred specialists. A psychologist who wishes to subcapitate or contract on a fee-for-service basis with another practitioner should model the posible effects of such an arrangement. Again, it is critical to understand that a subcontracted practitioner now assumes financial risk for the covered services. A fee-for-service contract means that the controlling psychologist is financially responsible to pay for all services of the referred-to provider.

Exhibit 4 also illustrates the value that the controlling psychologist could receive if all inpatient and outpatient services were provided through a single contract. In this case the controlling psychologist would receive $6.01 PMPM. Substantial savings can be achieved if the psychologist and any contracted specialists can control inpatient costs and utilization rates. By controlling the capitation rate for the full continuum of services, the psychologist can structure the rules, guidelines, and critical pathways for care. If more outpatient services are required, the savings from inpatient care can be applied to cover additional outpatient services. The system, as controlled by the psychologist, may allocate funds to whatever services are appropriate. The tradeoff is that the psychologist is also at financial risk if care is provided beyond the utilization and cost assumptions built into the capitation rate.

The services performed under any contract may be shared by two or more providers. That is, the values given in Exhibit 4 are for a single psychologist. But to serve an entire geographical area and provide multispecialty psychological services, several psychologists may be involved for a smaller percentage of their practices. That is, 10 psychologists may each take 10% of the encounters generated by the 5,026 members. Thus, the question becomes: if multiple practitioners provide services to the 5,026 members, how will revenues (the capitated premiums) be allocated? Allocation of the capitation rate may be based on member selection by the psychologist, random alphabetical assignment, or another process that splits the membership among the psychologists. Member selection means that the beneficiary chooses his or her practitioner and the administrator of the capitated premium allocates revenue for each provider by the number of covered patients who selected him or her as their provider. For example, if 2,500 members select Dr. Jones, revenues would equal 2,500 × $1.64, or $4,100 per month. Similarly, allocation could be based on alphabetical listings. For example, Dr. Jones may be responsible to provide services to all members whose last names begin with the letters A through F. The same could be done with ZIP codes: anyone whose ZIP code begins with a 1, 2, or 3 would see Dr. Jones. In other words, virtually any random allocation of the covered population would suffice. The key is to ensure randomness so that no one practitioner is singled out to provide services to that portion of the population with the highest activity level.

Exhibit 5 shows the capitation PMPM for an HMO managed care system. The type of managed care system will affect the actuarial assumptions. For example, HMOs typically have younger members who seek fewer psychological services. In addition, more supportive emotional care may be provided by the PCP or "gatekeeper" than is typical under a fee-for-service arrangement. In an HMO some of the lower inpatient costs are generated by the encouragement to substitute outpatient services for some inpatient care. However, in HMOs it typically takes more members to generate the same number of visits to a psychologist than under a PPO contract. Also, because of the exclusive nature of the HMO (i.e., no out-of-network benefits for patients), many psychologists are willing to offer lower reimbursement rates. An example of what capitation rates might be with an HMO is given in Exhibit 5.

In this case a psychologist may decide to take a reduced capitation rate of $1.40 PMPM (less than the $1.64 PMPM capitation rate under the PPO contract). Or the psychologist may realize that a broader contracting arrangement might allow more control over finances and structure the use of services among psychologists, psychiatrists, inpatient hospitals, and other providers.

More restrictive and exclusive managed behavioral health care services generally mean lower PMPMs for psychologists. Most excess services have already been eliminated, as reflected by the low capitation rates. Therefore, the psychologist is left with the reality of surviving in the current market, creating market demand for expanded services, or shifting costs further from other providers to cover psychologist services.

Exhibit 6 shows expected outpatient psychological services by age group for a PPO with 1,361 annual patient visits. If a psychologist specializes in child, adolescent, or adult care only, a larger membership group is required before an adequate number of visits is generated to occupy the psychologist on a full-time basis because the psychologist's services are so specialized and pertain to a limited population.

The numbers in Exhibit 6 are based on reasonable expectations and illustrate expected utilization rates for services by age groups. If a psychologist practices only in one segment, the managed care membership needed

EXHIBIT 5   HMO Capitation per Member per Month

	Total Revenues	Copayment Revenues	Capitation Revenues	Capitation PMPM
Psychologist's services	$123,851	$35,220	$88,631	$1.40
All outpatient services	$177,164	$50,315	$126,849	$2.00
All inpatient and outpatient services	$340,074	$78,897	$261,177	$4.12

Source: Coopers & Lybrand.

to generate 1,361 visits will be larger. For example, if the psychologist works only with children (ages 0–12), it would take a total membership base of 76,988 to create enough patients to occupy the psychologist in a given year.

Exhibit 7 shows the number of full-time equivalent (FTE) psycholo-

EXHIBIT 6   PPO Utilization by Age Group

	Annual Treatments per 1,000 Members	Average No. of Visits per Treatment	Average No. of Vists per 1,000 Members	Membership of Age Group Served	Total Membership
All Ages	27.6	9.8	271	5,026	5,026
Children (ages 0–12)	10.8	9.1	98	13,858	76,988
Adolescents (ages 13–17)	25.3	9.1	230	5,911	84,445
Adults (ages 18 and over)	28.2	11.2	316	4,307	5,742

Source: Coopers & Lybrand.

gists needed to provide outpatient psychological services to various-sized populations for a PPO with 1,361 annual visits per psychologist and 271 visits per 1,000 members. This exhibit gives an indication of the number of practitioner contracts necessary to meet the needs of a given population if, on average, the managed care contract represents 10% of each psychologist's practice.

As groups of psychologists join together to develop integrated delivery systems for behavioral health care, similar calculations will be necessary so that the network can contract with enough practitioners to meet the service and access needs of the total membership population. The geographical locations of members and practitioners as well as specialty types may affect the distribution of business among the practitioners.

Exhibit 8 shows the number of FTEs required to meet the behavioral health care outpatient needs of an employer with 40,000 employees, in a PPO with 1,361 annual visits per psychologist and 271 visits per 1,000 members.

If a group of psychologists decides to bid on a capitated contract, the

EXHIBIT 7   Required Number of Full-Time Equivalent Psychologists

No. of Employees	No. of Members	Expected No. of Visits	Required No. of FTE Psychologists	Required No. of Contracts at 10% of Each Contract
500	1,250	339	0.2	2
1,000	2,500	677	0.5	5
2,000	5,000	1,355	1	10
5,000	12,500	3,386	2.5	25.3
10,000	25,000	6,773	5	50
15,000	37,500	10,159	7.5	75
20,000	50,000	13,545	9.9	99
25,000	62,500	16,931	12.4	124
40,000	100,000	27,090	19.9	199
50,000	125,000	33,863	24.9	249
75,000	187,500	50,794	37.3	373
100,000	250,000	67,725	49.7	497

Source: Coopers & Lybrand.

EXHIBIT 8   Required Number of Psychologists for 100,000 Members by Age

	No. of Members	Expected No. of Visits	Required No. of FTE Psychologists	Required No. of Contracts at 10% of Each Practice
Children (0–12)	18,000	1,768	1.3	13
Adolescents (13–17)	7,000	1,612	1.2	12
Adults (18+)	75,000	23,710	17.4	174
All ages	100,000	27,090	19.9	199

Source: Coopers & Lybrand.

above analysis gives an indication of the number of contracts required to meet the service needs. Should the contracting psychologists build their practices around the contract, only 20 psychologists are needed. However, geographical requirements or restraints may demand some contracting with additional psychologists. A population of 100,000 requires only 20 full-time psychologists. If psychologists do not take control and ownership of the membership, someone else is likely to determine where that patient population will receive care.

CAPITATION BY BUILDUP BY CPT SERVICES METHOD

Another procedure to follow in calculating an appropriate capitation rate for a specific practice is to review an existing contract of similar members and the services utilized by them over a 12-month period. Psychologists may be able to take their own practice experience and account for the assumptions needed to determine a capitation rate by the Buildup by CPT Services Method.

Exhibit 9 shows the calculation of a capitation by a "buildup" method. That is, specific key CPT codes are used to define the practice. The number of services provided and the price charged for each service are determined. The average patient portion of the service payment can be estimated by reviewing the psychologist's insurance records. Payment records or Explanation of Benefits statements from insurance carriers can be sampled to estimate aggregate patient and plan payment percentages of total charges.

Gross revenue is determined by multiplying the number of services per year by the fee per service. The total copayment per service is assumed to average $25 per encounter times the number of services per year. The net insured payment is the gross revenue less the total copayment per service.

Using the above assumptions, the net insured payment converts to an annual capitation rate per member by dividing the net insured payment by the number of members ($120,000 ÷ 5,000 = $24.00). The monthly capitation or PMPM value of $2.00 is the annual capitation divided by 12 months ($24.00 ÷ 12 = $2.00).

MARKET ANALYSIS METHOD

Some psychologists may lack the basic statistical information to develop capitation rates based on an analysis of their own practice needs and data. In such cases a psychologist should gather as much information as possible on current contracts in the local marketplace. Although this approach has substantial inadequacies, it can be used to obtain data on initial experience with capitation contracting. HMOs and insurance carriers are generally required to file the rate structure for their products with state insurance commissioners. Some states require filing for approval by the commissioner, while others require filing for information purposes only. In either case, such filings are public information available for review on request.

In many filings, detailed information is included on utilization assumptions and costs. Separate premium developments also may be detailed in the filings for specialty areas such as behavioral health and substance abuse benefits. While capitation is the term used for fixed monthly amounts paid to providers, premiums are the amounts paid to insurers or HMOs. If only premiums are available in the filing information, the psychologist may estimate the capitation claims cost by removing an amount for the HMO's administrative/marketing/profit expense components. Typical expenses are 15 to 25% of the premium. The psychologist can multiply the HMO premium by .85 or .75 to determine the capitation claims cost. The higher

EXHIBIT 9 Simplified Practice Analysis (5,000 Members)

CPT Code	Service Description	No. of Services per Year	Fee per Service	Gross Revenue	$25 Copayment per Service	Net Insured Payment
90801	Psychiatric Interview	40	$150	$6,000	$1,000	$5,000
90843	Psychotherapy (20–30 min)	80	$75	$6,000	$2,000	$4,000
90844	Psychotherapy (45–50 min)	1,000	$132	$132,000	$25,000	$107,000
90853	Group therapy	80	$75	$6,000	$2,000	$4,000
Total				$150,000	$30,000	$120,000
Annual Capitation per Member				$30.00	$6.00	$24.00
Monthly Capitation PMPM				$2.50	$ .50	$2.00

value of .85 should be used if the HMO has delegated substantial administrative and marketing services to its providers or the integrated delivery system. It may be necessary to ask the HMO that is providing the claims administration, marketing, and other administrative services to make this judgment. The lower value of .75 should be used if the providers are mainly supplying clinical services while the HMO supplies administrative, reporting, case management, and marketing services.

Developing a profile of HMO behavioral health premium and cost assumptions from previous rate filings will give a market-based indication for competitive bids. The psychologist must be cautious in the application of the rate filing information to specific cases, large employer groups, or blocks of business controlled by managed behavioral health care companies. Many factors, such as age, sex, underwriting standards, plan design, and utilization management, affect the calculations. However, if no other basis for determining capitation is available, the psychologist can establish reasonable parameters for judging the current market payments for behavioral health care services.

This process can be used for limited contracting when a psychologist is considering a capitation arrangement that will be less than 10% of his or her patient base. By negotiating certain limits on patient load from any single capitated arrangement, the psychologist may be able to gain confidence in the relationship before expanding further into arrangements with the managed care organization.

ADDITIONAL RESOURCES

Actuaries provide capitation calculations to the HMO and insurance industry. Actuaries can assist in requesting the correct information, analyzing data, modeling capitation parameters, and negotiating contracts. A psychologist, group practice, or integrated delivery system can obtain the same expertise by hiring actuarial consultants. Specific behavioral health care models are available. Caution should be used in interpreting the results because local conditions and additional factors may significantly influence the final capitation.

OTHER APPROACHES TO CAPITATION

In many markets, capitation is still a new payment approach. Usually, managed care organizations realize the need to transition providers into these arrangements. As such, a capitated contract may include an initial period of monitoring services provided on a discounted fee-for-service basis. After an agreed-upon time period of 6 months to a year, the agreement then converts to a capitated arrangement based on the utilization experience recorded during the test period.

Another approach is to convert to a capitated arrangement once membership or patient volume reaches a critical, sustainable, and credible level. This approach is most desirable for the establishment of true partnerships between providers and managed care organization. By allowing for a transition period, a provider can gauge the compatibility of his or her relationship with the managed care organization, judge the quality and utilization control implications of capitation, and make informed decisions based on that experience.

Once the data are available, the Aggregate Time Method or the Buildup by CPT Services Method can be used to establish the required capitation rate. It is still important to gather market information to competitively set capitation rates regardless of the experience data. A psychologist may want higher capitations, but employers and members choose plans based largely on premiums. High capitations may mean high premiums, and high premiums may mean fewer members. Fewer members and small market share will lower a provider's income more rapidly than low capitation rates.

LOADS TO CAPITATION CLAIMS COSTS

In addition to the cost of providing psychological services, most capitation calculations are adjusted to reflect the age and sex mix of the membership, the administrative responsibilities required of the capitated provider(s), the need for protection against large claims on any one individual (stop-loss/catastrophic insurance), and some means of accounting for uncertainty and normal fluctuations in the number of claims.

These adjustments can be demonstrated by using the values from the Buildup by CPT Services Method in calculating capitation claims costs. Once the monthly capitation value is determined, the following adjustments may be considered in the negotiations:

Monthly capitation (PMPM): $2.00
Administration expenses (3% of PMPM)*: .06

Stop-loss/catastrophic insurance (6% of PMPM)*   .12
Margin (5% of PMPM)*:   .10
Total PMPM capitation   2.28
*Though these values are common, actual rates should be negotiated based on the services provided.

In addition, the monthly capitation rate may reflect the demographics of the membership. Separate age and sex factors for behavioral health care services are not well established. Most demographic adjustments are made to a plan's overall benefits. A sample list of age and sex factors that can be applied to a behavioral health care capitation contract is illustrated in Exhibit 10.

To use the age and sex factors in Exhibit 10, multiply the proposed membership population by the appropriate factors. Add all values together and divide the sum by the total number of enrolled members. Multiply the capitation claims cost by the resulting factor. Perform this calculation separately for the age factor and the sex factor. The answer provides an adjustment to reflect the capitation required for a population that varies from a normal distribution of membership demographics. That is, this adjustment allows a psychologist to increase or decrease the capitation to reflect higher or lower ages and more male or female members than otherwise expected. See Exhibit 11 for an example.

Other adjustments may be needed to reflect variations from normally expected utilization. Among the concerns usually considered in an actuarial analysis of capitation rates are:

EXHIBIT 10   Example: Demographic Factors for Utilization

	Inpatient Services	Outpatient Services
By Age		
Less than 15	0.37	0.45
15–24	1.04	0.74
25–44	1.51	1.42
45–64	1.02	1.30
65 and over	0.93	0.48
By sex		
Male	0.97	0.88
Female	1.03	1.11

EXHIBIT 11   Example: Age and Sex Factors Included in the Capitation Rate

Number of members: 5,000

Sex factors (inpatient services)

	No. of Members (A)	Sex Factor (B)	Sex Adjustment (C = A x B)	Capitation Adjustment Factor (C ÷ A)
Male	3,000	0.97	2,910	
Female	2,000	1.03	2,060	
Total	5,000		4,970	0.99

Age factors (inpatient services):

	No. of Members (A)	Sex Factor (B)	Sex Adjustment (C = A x B)	Capitation Adjustment Factor (C ÷ A)
< 15	50	0.37	18.50	
15–24	500	1.04	520	
25–44	2,500	1.51	3,775	
45–64	1,200	1.02	1,224	
65 and over	750	0.93	697.5	
Total	5,000		6,235	1.25

Adjusted capitation rate:

Capitation Claims Cost (PMPM) (A)	Capitation Adjustment Factor for Sex (B)	Capitation Adjustment Factor for Age (C)	Adjusted Capitation Rate (A x B x C)
$2.00	0.99	1.25	$2.48

- geographical differences,
- accepted local behavioral health practice patterns,
- specialty services provided,

- plan design,
- case management program effectiveness, and
- employee education.

Actual PMPM rates vary significantly depending on the services covered by a contract and the historical utilization rates of the enrolled population. For example, the rate a psychologist receives may or may not include reimbursement for certain tests or assessments. Rates differ depending on what services are covered under each capitation rate. Capitation rates are typically higher when providers are new to capitation than when they have experience with managed care. This is due to historical experience and utilization as well as a provider's overall comfort with a capitation arrangement.

Capitation rates may vary from region to region and from practice to practice, depending on the scope of services allocated to each specialty. Instead of having a flat rate PMPM for all specialties across regions or practices, rates are customized and presumably fair for all providers involved. According to a survey of 320 HMOs nationwide (which represented 62% of the commercial HMO population), obstetrics/gynecology and radiology were the specialties with the highest average PMPM capitation rate (see Table 11). Psychology ranked fourth.

TRACKING CLAIMS EXPERIENCE UNDER CAPITATION

Once a capitation rate has been determined, a psychologist will need to track his or her utilization experience in a manner similar to the one used by the managed care organization. Usually, the managed care organization will supply information periodically to the practitioner. This information documents actual versus expected utilization rates and costs. A fee-for-service equivalent database is tracked to compare the capitation results to costs otherwise expected when a provider delivers services on a fee-for-service basis. Since the financial incentives for fee-for-service arrangements and capitation are so different, it is possible to determine whether a provider is actually delivering care at the most appropriate level. Reporting of this information may follow the same time delays or "claims lags" of traditional fee-for-service arrangements. In an integrated delivery system, not all providers will be subcapitated. Actuarial studies of claims lags are used to analyze the developing experience of practitioners who are capitated.

Exhibit 12 gives an example of claims data from the month a service

TABLE 11 Average Physician Payments (Commercial Population) by Specialty

	Average PMPM Capitation Rate
Ob/gyn	$2.305
Radiology	$1.910
Anesthesiology	$1.771
Psychiatry/psychology	$1.671
Orthopedics	$1.159
General surgery	$1.101
Ophthalmology	$0.695
Cardiology	$0.636
Urology	$0.497
Cardiology (invasive)	$0.361
Oncology	$0.274
Neurology	$0.264

Source: *The HMO Executive Salary Survey*, Warren Surveys, Rockford, IL, 1993.

was performed to the month the payment was processed. Using these historical relationships, the developing experience can be translated into a capitation rate PMPM for comparison purposes. The main point of this analysis is to adjust the developing paid experience for the cost of services that have already been provided with the service costs that have been incurred but not yet reported (IBNR).

Without the adjustment for IBNR, the PMPM capitation rate is $1.58. This might lead the provider who is accepting a $2.00 PMPM to believe the experience is favorable. Using this information only, the provider might be willing to lower the capitation rate during a renewal discussion. However, with full recognition of additional services provided but not yet processed, the actual PMPM is estimated at $2.22, which shows experience that is more than 10% above the $2.00 contracted rate.

Based on these cost and utilization assumptions, the practitioner may argue for an increased capitation rate at renewal time. The IBNR amounts can be derived by actuarial analyses of the historical patterns of the claims lags. The percentage of claims processed within 1 to 3 months from the month the service was performed can be determined. These values are then applied as "completion factors" to the known claims. The managed care organization can supply the psychologist with completion factors and/or the total IBNR reserves on request. For practitioner-owned systems taking on financial risk, the determination of reserves requires an actuarial

EXHIBIT 12 Claims Experience

Month Paid	Month Service Was Performed						
	January	February	March	April	May	June	Total
January	$ 1,000						$ 1,000
February	15,000	$ 2,000					17,000
March	30,000	22,000	$ 1,000				53,000
April	5,000	4,000	28,000	3,000			40,000
May	1,000	4,000	8,000	32,000	2,000		47,000
June	0	2,000	5,000	15,000	30,000	1,000	53,000
Total paid claims	$52,000	$34,000	$42,000	$50,000	$32,000	$ 1,000	$211,000
No. of members	20,000	21,000	22,000	23,000	24,000	24,000	134,000
Paid PMPM	$ 2.60	$ 1.62	$ 1.91	$ 2.17	$ 1.33	$ .04	$ 1.58
IBNR reserves*	$ 1,000	$ 3,000	$ 4,000	$ 8,000	$18,000	$52,000	$ 86,000
Incurred claims	$53,000	$37,000	$46,000	$58,000	$50,000	$53,000	$297,000
Incurred PMPM	$ 2.65	$ 1.76	$ 2.09	$ 2.52	$ 2.08	$ 2.21	$ 2.22

*IBNR = Incurred but not reported.

certification. Actuarial analyses can be purchased from various consulting organizations.

In addition to tracking each practitioner's utilization rates and costs, it is important to track the following:

- inpatient admissions and lengths of stay;
- frequency of the use of alternative facilities such as partial hospitalization and day programs;
- referral sources (e.g., primary care providers) or self-referred patients;
- types of testing and assessment procedures;
- number of visits for a completed treatment;
- referrals to specialists;
- number of patients requiring medication management;
- number of patients exceeding plan benefits;
- out-of-area emergency costs;
- patient copayments;
- uncollected payments; and
- payments disputed due to ineligible membership.

Depending on the managed care organization the psychologist is contracting with, some or all of this information may be available if the managed care oganization profiles providers. Practitioners should also receive patient satisfaction surveys developed by the managed care organization. To the extent that a psychologist will need to track this information, additional administrative charges should be built into the capitation rate.

SUMMARY

Capitation is a reimbursement arrangement whereby providers are prepaid for services that may be needed by a defined membership population. Mathematically, capitation is frequency times cost. Frequency is usually stated in terms of services per 1,000 members. Frequency can itself involve multiple considerations. For example, outpatient psychological frequency can be expressed as an admission rate per 1,000 members (number of patients beginning treatment) times the average length of treatment in order to calculate the total number of outpatient visits per 1,000 members. The number of visits per 1,000 multiplied by the cost per visit is the key component of a capitation calculation. Costs are the payments made by the insurance plan for covered and eligible charges.

Several methods can be used to estimate an appropriate capitation rate for a given practice. The initial step is calculation of a capitation claims cost. The claims cost is that portion of the capitation required to cover the pure clinical services of the psychologist. Amounts in addition to the capitation claims cost are part of the contract analysis and negotiations. For example, additional capitation should be requested if new and expensive administrative functions are required. Protection from individual catastrophic claims also will mean an additional load.

The Aggregate Time Analysis Method allows a psychologist to value his or her practice time with an understanding of the limited amount available for charging services. The Buildup by CPT Services Method creates a modeling process of the actual services rendered by the psychologist. The Market Analysis Method provides a reality check and a due diligence comparison to actual rate filings made by managed care organizations.

An alternative may be an HMO partner that is willing to share data and utilization information from its membership population. If a practice lacks good data, a transition period of 6 to 12 months may be negotiated so that capitation can be based on agreed-upon standards.

Once a capitation or other risk-sharing contract is in place, it is important for the provider to closely monitor the developing results. An actuarial analysis that includes a claims-lag analysis may prove helpful in early detection of an inadequate capitation rate. Such tracking will also be needed for renewal negotiations. If experience analysis is not done properly, delays in processing of claims may distort renewal reporting and lead to inadequate renewal capitation rates.

5

Sample Capitation
Rates for Typical Plan Designs

T HIS CHAPTER PRESENTS *sample capitation claims rates for various plan designs typically sold by insurers and HMOs. These values are illustrative only. Various factors may affect a practice's actual experience with a given contract. Age, sex, local practices, benefits history, and other factors have a substantial impact on capitation calculations. The values given here are for average age, sex, and industry factors. The average negotiated fees are projected for the period January 1, 1996, through December 31, 1996. Each psychologist may negotiate specific issues when contracting with a managed care organization. These sample values provide an idea of the rates that can be expected. There may not necessarily be a logical relationship between historical costs, actual costs, and negotiated managed care fees. Psychologists are advised to seek professional legal, accounting, tax, or actuarial assistance before accepting or rejecting a capitated agreement.*

MANAGED CARE SYSTEMS

Capitation rates are given in Tables 12, 13, and 14 for three general types of health care delivery systems—commercial HMO, PPO, and managed indemnity system—respectively. In any given market, there are significant differences among HMOs for which these sample capitation rates cannot differentiate. The HMO, PPO, and managed indemnity designs are used to describe the type of capitation rates generally associated with a particular plan type. The different system designs also describe how behavioral health care services are typically managed in each type.

A psychologist considering an HMO arrangement can refer to Table 12 for capitation rates under typical plan designs. Under these designs with various behavioral health care benefits limits and copayments, a psychologist can expect capitation rates to range from $3.87 PMPM to $6.21.

None of these approaches assumes heavy outpatient utilization review for psychological services since there is no evidence that restrictive outpatient reviews and approvals for as few as three to five visits are cost effective, although this still takes place in some areas. The added administrative burden and reviewer charges do not generate any cost savings from fewer outpatient visits. Outpatient services are encouraged since they incur the lowest costs for many treatment programs and increase customer satisfaction. Any provider abuses are assumed to be identified under retrospective reviews. A provider may be asked to leave the PPO or HMO network if his or her overall standards and care guidelines are not consistent with the cost and quality concerns of the managed care organization.

A managed indemnity plan is similar to a traditional indemnity or fee-for-service arrangement. The difference is that it involves increased cost control or management of services by the plan. To oversee the lack of a defined network of providers and the total freedom of choice in a traditional fee-for-service design, employers implement utilization review and inpatient hospital precertification procedures. For psychologists these procedures are administered by utilization review personnel who specialize in behavioral health.

Managed indemnity plans focus on inpatient hospital reviews more than on outpatient reviews. The procedures are limited and specific to behavioral health care and assume more than the use of behavioral health care professionals to make utilization decisions regarding payment for services.

A psychologist who is considering negotiating with a managed indemnity plan in which there are self-referrals and freedom of choice among providers for members should refer to Table 14. Under a managed indemnity plan, the psychologist can gain a better idea of the capitation rates based on a typical plan design of behavioral health care benefit limits and coinsurance. Under a typical plan design illustrated in Table 14, capitation rates vary from $5.78 per member per month (PMPM) to $10.34 PMPM. The rates depend on the benefits and coinsurance of the plan design.

A PPO consists of providers who have agreed to participate in a managed care network and discount their fees in exchange for increased patient volume. Participants may choose any practitioner, hospital, or alternative care facility, but a higher payment percentage is allowed for ser-

TABLE 12 Example: Capitation Claims Costs for a Commercial HMO, January–December 1996

Annual Limit on Benefits			Cost Sharing by Patient			Capitation Claims Costs PMPM			Total Capitation Claims Cost PMPM
Inpatient Hospital	Partial Hospital	Outpatient	Inpatient Hospital ($)	Partial Hospital ($)	Outpatient ($)	Inpatient Hospital ($)	Partial Hospital ($)	Outpatient ($)	Claims Cost PMPM ($)
30 Days	30 Days	30 Visits	0/Day	0/Day	0/Visit	2.45	0.46	2.54	5.45
					5/Visit	2.45	0.46	2.34	5.25
					10/Visit	2.45	0.46	2.16	5.07
					15/Visit	2.45	0.46	1.99	4.90
					25/Visit	2.45	0.46	1.66	4.57
30 Days	30 Days	30 Visits	100/Day	50/Day	0/Visit	1.87	0.34	2.54	4.75
					5/Visit	1.87	0.34	2.34	4.55
					10/Visit	1.87	0.34	2.16	4.37
					15/Visit	1.87	0.34	1.99	4.20
					25/Visit	1.87	0.34	1.66	3.87
30 Days	30 Days	Unlimited	0/Day	0/Day	0/Visit	2.41	0.46	3.08	5.95
					5/Visit	2.41	0.46	2.83	5.70
					10/Visit	2.41	0.46	2.58	5.45
					15/Visit	2.41	0.46	2.35	5.22
					25/Visit	2.41	0.46	1.94	4.81
30 Days	30 Days	Unlimited	100/Day	50/Day	0/Visit	1.84	0.34	3.08	5.26
					5/Visit	1.84	0.34	2.83	5.01
					10/Visit	1.84	0.34	2.58	4.76
					15/Visit	1.84	0.34	2.35	4.53
					25/Visit	1.84	0.34	1.94	4.12

				0/Visit	5/Visit	10/Visit	15/Visit	25/Visit

45 Days	30 Visits	0/Day	0/Day					
			0/Visit	2.66	0.51	2.54	5.71	
			5/Visit	2.66	0.51	2.34	5.51	
			10/Visit	2.66	0.51	2.16	5.33	
			15/Visit	2.66	0.51	1.99	5.16	
			25/Visit	2.66	0.51	1.66	4.83	

45 Days	30 Visits	100/Day	50/Day					
			0/Visit	2.00	0.37	2.54	4.91	
			5/Visit	2.00	0.37	2.34	4.71	
			10/Visit	2.00	0.37	2.16	4.53	
			15/Visit	2.00	0.37	1.99	4.36	
			25/Visit	2.00	0.37	1.66	4.03	

45 Days	45 Visits	0/Day	0/Day					
			0/Visit	2.62	0.51	2.80	5.93	
			5/Visit	2.62	0.51	2.58	5.71	
			10/Visit	2.62	0.51	2.37	5.50	
			15/Visit	2.62	0.51	2.17	5.30	
			25/Visit	2.62	0.51	1.80	4.93	

45 Days	45 Visits	100/Day	50/Day					
			0/Visit	1.97	0.37	2.80	5.14	
			5/Visit	1.97	0.37	2.58	4.92	
			10/Visit	1.97	0.37	2.37	4.71	
			15/Visit	1.97	0.37	2.17	4.51	
			25/Visit	1.97	0.37	1.80	4.14	

45 Days	Unlimited	0/Day	0/Day					
			0/Visit	2.62	0.51	3.08	6.21	
			5/Visit	2.62	0.51	2.83	5.96	
			10/Visit	2.62	0.51	2.58	5.71	
			15/Visit	2.62	0.51	2.35	5.48	
			25/Visit	2.62	0.51	1.94	5.07	

45 Days	Unlimited	100/Day	50/Day					
			0/Visit	1.97	0.37	3.08	5.42	
			5/Visit	1.97	0.37	2.83	5.17	
			10/Visit	1.97	0.37	2.58	4.92	
			15/Visit	1.97	0.37	2.35	4.69	
			25/Visit	1.97	0.37	1.94	4.28	

TABLE 13 Example: Capitation Claims Costs for a Commercial PPO, January–December 1996

Annual Limit on Benefits			Cost Sharing by Patient			Capitation Claims Costs PMPM			Total Capitation
Inpatient Hospital	Partial Hospital	Outpatient	Inpatient Hospital (%)	Partial Hospital (%)	Outpatient (%)	Inpatient Hospital ($)	Partial Hospital ($)	Outpatient ($)	Claims Cost PMPM ($)
30 Days	30 Days	30 Visits	0	0	20	4.50	0.46	2.23	7.19
			20	20	20	3.11	0.32	2.23	5.66
			20	20	50	3.11	0.32	1.22	4.65
30 Days	30 Days	Unlimited	0	0	20	4.42	0.46	2.66	7.54
			20	20	20	3.06	0.32	2.66	6.04
			20	20	50	3.06	0.32	1.41	4.79
45 Days	45 Days	30 Visits	0	0	20	5.07	0.52	2.23	7.82
			20	20	20	3.44	0.36	2.23	6.03
			20	20	50	3.44	0.36	1.22	5.02
45 Days	45 Days	45 Visits	0	0	20	4.98	0.52	2.44	7.94
			20	20	20	3.39	0.36	2.44	6.19
			20	20	50	3.39	0.36	1.32	5.07
45 Days	45 Days	Unlimited	0	0	20	4.98	0.52	2.66	8.16
			20	20	20	3.38	0.36	2.66	6.40
			20	20	50	3.39	0.36	1.41	5.16

TABLE 14 Example: Capitation Claims Costs for a Commercial Managed Indemnity, January–December 1996

Annual Limit on Benefits			Cost Sharing by Patient			Capitation Claims Costs PMPM			Total Capitation Claims Costs PMPM ($)
Inpatient Hospital	Partial Hospital	Outpatient	Inpatient Hospital (%)	Partial Hospital (%)	Outpatient (%)	Inpatient Hospital ($)	Partial Hospital ($)	Outpatient ($)	Claims Costs PMPM ($)
30 Days	30 Days	30 Visits	0	0	20	6.25	0.46	2.31	9.02
			20	20	20	4.22	0.32	2.31	6.85
			20	20	50	4.22	0.32	1.24	5.78
30 Days	30 Days	Unlimited	0	0	20	6.13	0.46	2.75	9.34
			20	20	20	4.13	0.32	2.75	7.20
			20	20	50	4.13	0.32	1.43	5.88
45 Days	45 Days	30 Visits	0	0	20	7.21	0.53	2.31	10.05
			20	20	20	4.75	0.36	2.31	7.42
			20	20	50	4.75	0.36	1.24	6.35
45 Days	45 Days	45 Visits	0	0	20	7.06	0.53	2.52	10.11
			20	20	20	4.66	0.36	2.52	7.54
			20	20	50	4.66	0.36	1.34	6.36
45 Days	45 Days	Unlimited	0	0	20	7.06	0.53	2.75	10.34
			20	20	20	4.66	0.36	2.75	7.77
			20	20	50	4.66	0.36	1.43	6.45

vices provided by in-network providers. The higher reimbursements are designed to steer members to network providers without severely restraining their choices.

PPO designs generally call for tighter utilization controls, with participating physicians conceding some amount of fee reduction. Out-of-network services are allowed, but the financial penalty for such access offsets lower fees. The focus of utilization management is on inpatient and intensive outpatient behavioral health care services. A psychologist who is considering a PPO arrangement in which members can choose between an in-network psychologist or an out-of-network psychologist should refer to Table 13. Under the typical plan design illustrated there, psychologists can expect capitation rates to range from $4.65 PMPM to $8.16 PMPM. Again, the different capitation rates are attributable to the behavioral health care benefits limits and cost-sharing arrangements of the memebers.

POS plans are similar to PPOs. A psychologist who is considering contracting with a POS plan should use Table 13 as a reference.

The HMO structure is designed to provide health care to members in a cost-effective and cost-efficient way. To remain financially competitive, HMOs try to reduce inpatient utilization. HMOs control hospital access through strong utilization review practices and procedures and the use of primary care physicians ("gatekeepers"). Self-referrals are usually not allowed, and only network providers are reimbursed for providing covered services.

In many markets full capitation with integrated delivery systems and providers of behavioral health care services may generate capitation claims costs that are similar to those in Tables 12–14. However, as integrated delivery systems develop, additional reductions in claims costs may be possible with acceptable quality standards. Costs that are lower than the capitation rates shown are possible and exist in some markets around the country today.

PLAN DESIGN

Several plan designs are used to frame the range of capitation calculations. The HMO plans include copayments. The PPO and managed indemnity plans include coinsurance amounts. As psychologists contract with different entities, they will find the different types of plan designs that are common to these types of coverages. Limits on benefits are typically applied on an annual basis. Limits for inpatient hospitalization, partial hospitalization, and outpatient services also given are in the tables. Although many plan designs do not currently include coverage for partial hospitalization, it is included in the total capitation claims cost for illustrative purposes.

COST SHARING BY PATIENTS

Separate cost-sharing amounts for each benefit are shown in the tables. Outpatient copayments ranging from 0 to $25 are used to estimate the impact on the capitation rate for a wide range of cost-sharing arrangements common in HMO plan designs.

Inpatient hospital copayments vary substantially from market to market. Many HMOs do not have copayments for inpatient behavioral health care services. Where cost sharing exists, a daily copayment or a per-admission copayment is included in HMO plans. The table with HMO capitations applies either a $100 per-day-copayment or no copayment for inpatient hospital coverage. HMO partial hospitalization coverage includes copayments ranging from 0 to $50 a day.

PPO and managed indemnity plans include coinsurance arrangements in which the patient pays a percentage of the charges. The tables include a range of assumptions for inpatient coverage, from no coinsurance (patient pays nothing, plan pays 100%) to 20% coinsurance (patient pays 20%, plan pays 80%).

Outpatient coverage under PPO and managed indemnity plans has been calculated by using coinsurance rates of 20% (plan pays 80%) and 50% (plan pays 50%), respectively.

CAPITATION CLAIMS COSTS PMPM

Capitation claims costs are the amounts charged on a capitated basis for all behavioral health care services. The claims cost amount may be increased for administrative costs associated with capitation, stop-loss coverage, and a margin for experience fluctuation. The ability to negotiate the needed claims cost plus administrative costs is likely to depend on the psychologist's business acumen or consulting support.

While separate inpatient, partial, and outpatient capitations are shown, each contract may include guidelines that create a local distinction in shifting services between modalities. The total capitation claims cost is more accurate than any individual part. Shifting capitations between inpatient and outpatient coverages depends on the overall structure and management of the managed care network. As an outpatient practitioner, caution should be taken to establish any potential shifting of patients from inpatient to outpatient care and the determination of how patients with behavioral health care needs will be handled by the primary care provider.

Tables 12–14 are *not* to be used in contract negotiations. They are presented here as reasonable and appropriate average capitations for various plan designs. It is important for psychologists to understand the relationship of a plan's design and the delivery system on capitation rates. The American Psychological Association has distributed modeling software to state associations for use in education and analysis of state health care reform activities. For an alternative plan design not shown in the tables, check with your state association or the APA for assistance. It is recommended that proper legal, actuarial, and other professional assistance be obtained before accepting or rejecting a contract.

Glossary

ACCESS Patients' ability to obtain needed health services. Measures of access include the location of health facilities and their hours of operation, patient travel time and distance to health facilities, the availability of medical services, and the cost of care.

CAPITATION Method of payment for health care services in which the provider accepts a fixed amount of payment per subscriber, per period of time, in return for specified services over a specified period of time.

CARRIER Any commercial insurance company.

CARVE OUT An arrangement in which coverage for a specific category of services (e.g., mental health/substance abuse, vision care, prescription drugs) is provided through a contract with a separate set of providers. The contract may specify certain payment and utilization management arrangements.

CASE MANAGEMENT Monitoring, planning, and coordination of treatment rendered to patients with conditions that are expected to require high cost or extensive services. Case management is focused and longitudinal, usually following the patient for 3 to 6 months minimum to avoid hsopital readmission.

Central Processing Unit (CPU) The computer's brain, which largely determines the speed and cost of hardware.

CLAIMS REVIEW A review of claims by government, medical foundations, professional review organizations, insurers, or others responsible for payment to determine liability and amount of payment.

CONCURRENT REVIEW Third party review of the medical necessity, level of care, length of stay, appropriateness of services, and discharge plan for a patient in a health care facility. Occurs at the time the patient is treated.

CONTINUUM OF CARE In behavioral health, generally defined as the spectrum of care delivered in residential treatment, inpatient, partial hospitalization, home health, and outpatient settings.

COPAYMENT   Type of cost sharing whereby insured or covered person pays a specified flat fee per unit of service or unit of time (e.g., $10 per office visit, $25 per inpatient hospital day); insurance covers the remainder of the cost.

COST CONTAINMENT   Actions taken by employers and insurers to curtail health care costs (e.g., increasing employee cost sharing, requiring second opinions, preadmission screening).

COST SHARING   Requirement that health care consumers contribute to their own medical care costs through deductibles and coinsurance or copayments.

CREDENTIALING   Process of reviewing a practitioner's credentials (i.e., training, experience, demonstrated ability) for the purpose of determining whether criteria for clinical privileges have been met.

DIAGNOSTIC RELATED GROUPS (DRGs)   Reimbursement methodology whereby hospitals receive a fixed fee per patient based on the admitting diagnosis regardless of the length of stay or amount of services received.

ENROLLMENT   Means by which a person establishes membership in a group insurance plan.

EXCESS CHARGES   Portion of any charge greater than the usual and prevailing charge for a service. A charge is "usual and prevailing" when it does not exceed the typical charge of the provider in the absence of insurance and when it is no greater than the general level of charges for comparable services and supplies made by other providers in the same area.

FEE FOR SERVICE   In the traditional fee-for-service model, the provider bills the patient or payer for a specified amount, typically on the basis of the amount of time spent delivering the service. Until recently, providers determined the fees charged for services and customary fees were generally accepted. Now, providers may be required to accept a payer's fee schedule, which demands that a certain fee be accepted as payment in full. PPOs represent an attempt to save the fee-for-service method of payment by regulating the cost of treatment in the context of a traditional reimbursement plan.

FEE SCHEDULE   A listing of accepted fees or predetermined monetary allowances for specified services and procedures.

FREE-STANDING FACILITY   Health care center that is physically separated from a hospital or other institution of which it is a legal part or with which it is affiliated, or an independently operated or owned private or public business or enterprise providing limited health care services or a range of services, such as ambulatory surgery, hemodialysis treatment, diagnostic tests, or examinations.

GATEKEEPING   Process by which a primary care provider directly provides primary care to patients and coordinates all diagnostic testing and specialty referrals required for patients' medical care. Referrals must be preauthorized by the gatekeeper unless there is an emergency. Gatekeeping is a subset of the functions of a primary provider's case manager.

GROUP CONTRACT   Arrangement between a managed care company and the subscribing group that contains rates, performance covenants, relationships among parties, schedule of benefits, and other conditions. The term is generally limited to a 12-month period but may be renewed.

GROUP PRACTICE   A group of practitioners organized as a private partnership, limited liability company, or corporation; participating practitioners share facilities and personnel as well as the earnings from their practice. The providers who make up a practice may represent either a single specialty or a range of specialties.

HEALTH MAINTENANCE ORGANIZATION (HMO)   Health care delivery system that provides comprehensive health services to an enrolled population frequently for a prepaid fixed (capitated) payment, although other payment arrangements can be made. The organization consists of a network of health care providers rendering a wide range of health services and assumes the financial risks of providing these services. Enrollees generally are not reimbursed for care provided outside the HMO network.

INDEMNITY INSURANCE PLAN   An insurance plan that pays specific dollar amounts to an insured individual for specific services and procedures without guaranteeing complete coverage for the full cost of health care services.

INDIVIDUAL PRACTICE ASSOCIATION (IPA) MODEL HMO   An organization that contracts with individual health care professionals to provide services in their own offices for enrollees of a health plan. Specialists are generally paid on a fee-for-service basis, but primary care providers may receive capitated payments.

INTEGRATED CARE   Alternative health care delivery system developed by the American Psychological Association in response to the rising cost of providing health care services. It is based on six concepts: Benefit Design, Case Management and Utilization Review, Communications, Direct Contracting, Network Development, and Outcomes.

INTEGRATED DELIVERY SYSTEM (IDS)   System of behavioral health care that offers "one-stop shopping" to potential payers, meaning that a payer can write one check for the entire delivery of care without having to independently negotiate terms with multiple unconnected providers. IDSs offer a full continuum of care, so patients and premiums are managed within one accountable plan's network of providers.

LEVERAGE   A managed care strategy for controlling costs by steering patients to lower-cost providers called substitutes. In behavioral health care, a clinical social worker's psychiatric nurse may be a substitute for a psychologist.

MANAGED CARE   A means of providing health care services in a defined network of health care providers who are given the responsibility to manage and provide quality, cost-effective care. Increasingly, the term is being used by many analysts to include (in addition to HMOs) PPOs and even forms of indemnity insurance coverage that incorporate preadmission certification and other utilization controls.

MENTAL HEALTH AND DRUG ABUSE SERVICES   There are three basic types of mental health services: inpatient care provided in short term psychiatric units in a general hospital or specialized psychiatric facility; outpatient care for individual or group counseling; and partial hospitalization, a combination of both of the above. See also Employee Assistance Program.

MONITOR   The video display portion of a computer system.

MSO   An entity that usually contracts with practitioner groups, independent practice associations, and medical foundations to provide a range of services required in medical practices, such as accounting, utilization review, and staffing.

MULTISPECIALTY GROUP   Group of doctors who represent various specialties and work together in a group practice.

NETWORK   Group of providers who mutually contract with carriers or employers to provide health care services to participants in a specified managed care plan. A contract determines the payment method and rates, utilization controls, and target utilization rates by plan participants.

NETWORKING To conect computer systems electronically so that users may share files or printers.

PEER REVIEW Evaluation by practicing providers (or other qualified professionals) of the quality and efficiency of services ordered or performed by other practicing providers. Medical practices, inpatient hospital and extended care facility analyses, utilization reviews, medical audits, ambulatory care, and claims reviews are all aspects of peer review.

PER DIEM Negotiated daily rate for delivery of all inpatient hospital services provided in one day regardless of the actual services provided. Per diems can also be developed by the type of care provided (e.g., one per diem rate for adult mental health, a different rate for adolescent substance abuse treatment).

PERFORMANCE STANDARDS Standards that an individual provider is expected to meet, especially with respect to quality of care. The standards may define the volume of care delivered in a specified time period.

PERIPHERALS Optional hardware devices that can be connected to a computer system via cables (e.g., a printer).

POOL A large number of small groups or individuals who are analyzed and rated as a single large group for insurance purposes. A risk pool may be any account that attempts to find the claims liability for a group with a common denominator.

PREADMISSION REVIEW When a provider requests that a patient be hospitalized, another opinion may be sought by the insurer. The second provider reviews the treatment plan, evaluates the patient's condition, and confirms the request for admission or recommends another course of action. Similar to second opinions on surgery.

PREAUTHORIZATION Review and approval of covered benefits, based on a provider's treatment plan. Some insurers require preauthorization for certain high-cost procedures. Others apply the preauthorization requirement when charges exceed a specified dollar amount.

PRECERTIFICATION Review of the necessity and length of a recommended hospital stay. Often, certification prior to admission is required for nonemergencies and within 48 hours of admission for emergency treatment.

PREFERRED PROVIDER ORGANIZATION (PPO) Selective contracting agreement with a specified network of health care providers at reduced or negotiated payment rates. In exchange for reduced rates, providers frequently receive expedited claims payments and/or a reasonably predictable market share of patients. Employees may have financial incentives to utilize PPO providers.

PROVIDER   Health care professional (or facility) licensed to provide one or more health care services to patients.

PROVIDER-HOSPITAL ORGANIZATION   Vertically integrated delivery system formed by practitioners and a hospital.

QUALITY ASSURANCE   Activities and programs intended to ensure the quality of care in a defined medical setting or program. Such programs include methods for documenting clinical practice, educational components intended to remedy identified deficiencies in quality, as well as the components necessary to identify and correct such deficiencies (such as peer or utilization review), and a formal process to assess a program's own effectiveness.

QUALITY MANAGEMENT   A participative intervention in which employees and managers continuously review the quality of the services they provide. The process identifies problems, tests solutions to those problems, and constantly monitors solutions for improvement.

REQUEST FOR PROPOSAL (RFP)   Formal document soliciting bids from system vendors.

RISK   The chance or possibility of loss. Risk sharing is often employed as a utilization control mechanism in HMOs. Risk is often defined in insurance terms as the possibility of loss associated with a given population.

SELECTIVE CONTRACTING   Negotiation by third-party payers of a limited number of contracts with health care professionals and facilities in a given service area. Preferential reimbursement practices and/or benefits are then offered to patients seeking care from these providers.

SOFTWARE   Computer programs used to instruct computer hardware on how to perform.

STAFF MODEL HMO   An HMO in which professional providers in a multi-specialty group are salaried employees of the HMO.

SUBSTITUTE   A provider who replaces another despite differences in training and licensing scope. A clinical social worker and a psychiatric nurse may be substitutes for each other.

SUPPORT   Assistance provided by a computer vendor after a sale, including training, maintenance, and trouble-shooting.

THIRD PARTY ADMINISTRATOR   Outside company responsible for handling claims and performing administrative tasks associated with health insurance plan maintenance.

THIRD-PARTY PAYER   An organization that pays or insures health care expenses on behalf of beneficiaries or recipients who pay premiums for such coverage.

USUAL, CUSTOMARY, AND REASONABLE (UCR)   Charges considered reasonable and that do not exceed those customarily charged for the same service by other providers in the area.

UTILIZATION REVIEW   Independent determination of whether health care services are appropriate and medically necessary on a prospective, concurrent, and/or retrospective basis to ensure that appropriate and necessary services are provided. Frequently used to curtail the provision of inappropriate services and/or to ensure that services are provided in the most cost-effective manner.

VALUE-BASED PURCHASING   Selection of a product or service based on criteria other than unit price. Value criteria may include quality, outcome, and access.

Bibliography

Corporate Leadership Council. (1995). *The third wave of health care cost savings: "Big hit" discounts from capital providers*. Washington, DC: The Advisory Board Company.

Data watch. (1995, January). *Business & Health, 13*(1), 18–19.

Data watch. (1995, February). *Business & Health, 13*(2), 18–19.

Data watch. (1995, May). *Business & Health, 13*(5), 19.

Dix, J. (1995, June). *HMO hot topics: Medicaid managed care opportunities*. Paper presented at the Society of Actuaries meeting, KPMG Peat Marwick, Vancouver, Canada.

Fasano, R. *Capitation success: Focusing on the older patients*. Paper presented at the Diversified Health Care Group meeting.

The Governance Committee. (1994). Research from around the nation. In *Capitation strategy* (pp. 10–29, 94–95). Washington, DC: The Advisory Board Company.

Group Health Association of America. (1994, November). *HMO industry profile* (1994 ed). Washington, DC: Author.

Lanman, R. R. (1995, June). Specialty care under capitation. In *Capitation success: Focusing on profitable management*. Seminar conducted at the meeting of the ADESSO Specialty Services Organization, Inc., San Mateo, CA.

Marion Merrell Dow. (1994). *Managed Care Digest* (HMO ed.) Kansas City, MO: author.

Marion Merrell Dow. (1995). The state of health care in America. *Business & Health, 13*(Suppl. C), 8–66.

McKell, D. C. (1995). *Capitation imperative: The final frontier*. Paper presented at Physicians Strategies 2000: Building Healthcare Partnerships Conference.

Rosenblatt, A. (1995, February). Actuarial and practical considerations in developing capitation rates. In *Capitation rate setting: An actuarial and financial workshop*. Workshop sponsored by Global Business Research, Ltd., New Orleans, LA.

Wrightson, C. W., Jr. (1990). Key features of the HMO concept. In *HMO rate setting & financial strategy* (pp. 30–52). Ann Arbor, MI: Health Administration Press Perspectives.